macOS Sonon

A Comprehensive Manual with Use   ...st
Version of macOS Sonoma and make   ...atures on Your
                        Ma

Perry
Hoover

Copyright © 2024 Perry Hoover

All rights reserved.

It is not legal to reproduce, duplicate, or transmit any part of this document by either electronic means or in printed format. Recording of this publication is strictly prohibited

Disclaimer

The information in this book is based on personal experience and anecdotal evidence. Although the author has made every attempt to achieve an accuracy of the information gathered in this book, they make no representation or warranties concerning the accuracy or completeness of the contents of this book. Your circumstances may not be suited to some illustrations in this book.

The author disclaims any liability arising directly or indirectly from the use of this book. Readers are encouraged to seek Medical. Accounting, legal, or professional help when required.

This guide is for informational purposes only, and the author does not accept any responsibilities for any liabilities resulting from the use of this information. While every attempt has been made to verify the information provided here, the author cannot assume any responsibility for errors, inaccuracies or omission.

Printed in the United States of America

Table of Contents

INTRODUCTION...i

CHAPTER ONE 1

A Review of macOS Sonoma and Its Features................. 1

How to Identify Your macOS Version............................. 7

Setting Up macOS Sonoma... 9

CHAPTER TWO 12

Start Using Apps 12

The Menu Bar 15

The Finder 20

Using Your Mouse or Trackpad................................... 25

Using the Keyboard 29

Taking Screenshots 31

CHAPTER THREE 35

Working with Windows 35

Customizing Window Tab Settings 37

Opening and Closing Apps... 38

Closing Apps on macOS Sonoma 39

Customizing App Settings 40

Finding Apps 41

Installing and Uninstalling Apps.................................. 43

Uninstalling Apps on macOS Sonoma........................ 44

Customizing App Settings 45

Customizing App Settings 48

CHAPTER FOUR 50

Navigating the Finder Window and Toolbar.................... 50

Accessing the Finder Window 51

Exploring the Finder Window 51

Customizing the Toolbar 52

Using the Search Function to Locate Files.................... 54

Viewing and Customizing the Path Bar........................ 57

Understanding the Path Bar 58

Adding File and Folder Shortcuts to the Toolbar 62

Customizing the Finder Toolbar for Quick Access....... 63

Utilizing the Preview Pane for Quick File Viewing 67

Exploring the Sidebar for Favorite Locations and Tags70

Syncing Files and Data Between Mac and Other
Devices 73

Keyboard Shortcuts for Efficient Finder Usage............ 76

Managing Files and Folders.. 78

Utilizing Finder Window Shortcuts 79

Finder Preferences and Settings................................... 80

Advanced Finder Tips and Tricks................................. 83

CHAPTER FIVE 88

Change Your Desktop Wallpaper.................................. 88

Customizing Your Wallpaper 90

Configuring Screen Saver Settings.................................. 92

Add Widgets to Your Desktop.. 93

Using Mission Control... 98

Managing Apps and Folders.. 104

Optimizing Your Dictation Experience........................... 108

CHAPTER SIX 110

Using Siri 110

Accessing Siri on Your Mac.. 111

Setting Up Siri on macOS Sonoma............................... 112

Using FaceTime for Video Calling................................ 114

Setting Up FaceTime for the First Time 115

FaceTime's Unique Features on macOS Sonoma 118

Enabling AirDrop on Your Mac...................................... 120

Accessing AirDrop on macOS Sonoma 121

Accessing Handoff on macOS Sonoma 125

Accessing Continuity Camera on macOS Sonoma . 130

Accessing Universal Clipboard on macOS Sonoma. 135

CHAPTER SEVEN 140

What is an Apple ID?.. 140

Set Up Your Apple ID.. 142

Set Up Family Sharing 150

Use Messages with Your Family 155

CHAPTER EIGHT 161

Open and Close Safari 161

Use Tabs to Manage Multiple Websites...... 170

CHAPTER NINE 177

Create and Organize Notes............................. 177

Embracing the Power of Multimedia........... 179

CHAPTER TEN 193

Send and Receive Emails 193

Setting Up Your Email Accounts.................. 194

Create and Organize Multiple Email Accounts........ 197

CHAPTER ELEVEN... 215

Import Photos from Your Camera or Phone.... 215

Edit Photos with Basic Tools......................... 224

Using Quick Look... 237

CHAPTER TWELVE 243

Create and Edit Documents with Pages....... 243

Create and Edit Spreadsheets with Numbers........ 259

Use Formulas and Functions for Calculations 264

CHAPTER THIRTEEN 274

Create and Edit Presentations with Keynotes...... 274

Use Animations and Transitions 284

CHAPTER FOURTEEN....................................... 293

Apple Music 293

Navigating the Apple Music Interface......... 294

Exploring Apple Music Radio 295

Navigating the Apple Books Interface......... 300

Apple Arcade 305

CHAPTER FIFTEEN 312

Keep macOS Sonoma Secure 312

Utilizing the Accessibility Features 318

CHAPTER SIXTEEN 322

Use a Printer on Your macOS Sonoma 322

Identifying and Resolving Common Issues on Your
macOS 332

Using the Built-In Troubleshooting Tools 336

Tips and Tricks on macOS Sonoma 340

CONCLUSION 346

ABOUT THE AUTHOR 348

INTRODUCTION

Welcome to your comprehensive guide to mastering the all-new macOS Sonoma. Apple's latest operating system for Mac computers brings a fresh look, enhanced features, and powerful capabilities to help you get more out of your device. Whether you're a long-time Mac user or new to Apple's ecosystem, this book will help you navigate Sonoma's interface like a pro.

It is designed with a step-by-step approach and will hold your hand through every aspect of the operating system, ensuring a smooth transition and efficient workflow. From customizing your desktop environment to exploring the revamped Finder, managing files and applications, and leveraging the power of advanced tools, we've got you covered.

But this guide isn't just about the technical details - it's about helping you develop an intuitive understanding of Sonoma's philosophy and design principles. With easy-to-follow explanations and real-world examples, you'll gain the confidence to tweak settings, install apps, and truly make your Mac experience your own.

Let's get started!

CHAPTER ONE

A Review of macOS Sonoma and Its Features

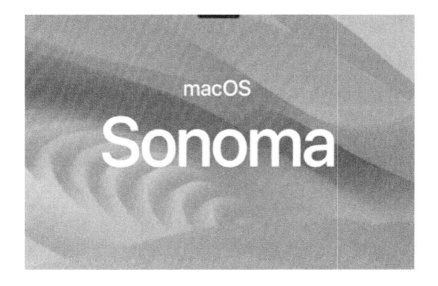

Apple's latest iteration of macOS, dubbed **"Sonoma,"** promises to elevate the desktop experience to unprecedented heights. With many innovative features and enhancements, this operating system update aims to redefine productivity, creativity, and user interaction. In this review, we look into the unique offerings of macOS Sonoma, uncovering how they harmonize to create a seamless and intuitive computing environment.

- **Visual Experience**

From the moment you boot up your Mac, macOS Sonoma captivates you with its stunning visual elements. Introducing high-resolution aerial views as desktop wallpapers and screen savers offers a breathtaking glimpse into the world's most picturesque landscapes. These dynamic visuals seamlessly transition between screen saver and wallpaper modes, creating a sense of immersion and tranquility that transcends mere aesthetics.

But the visual enhancements don't stop there. Sonoma introduces the highly anticipated Desktop Widgets, allowing users to place informative and interactive widgets directly on their desktops. Weather updates, calendars, and reminders are now just a glance away, fostering a more streamlined workflow and minimizing the need to switch between applications constantly.

- **Embracing the Era of Web Apps**

Apple's web browser, Safari, has undergone a significant overhaul in macOS Sonoma. Multiple profiles simultaneously empower users to manage distinct browsing contexts, separating personal and professional browsing experiences. This feature is precious for individuals juggling multiple online personas or valuing enhanced privacy and security.

Moreover, Web Apps take center stage in Sonoma, enabling users to create app-like experiences for their favorite websites. By seamlessly integrating web content into the macOS environment, users can enjoy a streamlined, immersive experience that blurs the lines between native and web applications.

- **Productivity with Preview and Notes**

macOS Sonoma's enhancements extend beyond visual aesthetics and web browsing, with significant improvements to core productivity applications like

Preview and Notes. In Preview, the introduction of separate markup tools specifically designed for filling in forms streamlines the process of completing PDFs with interactive fields. Gone are the days of cumbersome workarounds; you can now easily navigate and fill out complex forms.

The Notes app has also received a substantial update, introducing the ability to link between notes. This feature revolutionizes note-taking and organization, allowing users to create intricate webs of interconnected information. Whether cross-referencing research materials or organizing personal notes, this functionality empowers users to navigate their digital content with unparalleled efficiency.

Reminders, another essential productivity tool, has been enhanced with new list organization features. Users can now create sections within their lists, fostering better organization and clarity. Additionally, the auto-sectioning feature for grocery lists intelligently categorizes items, making shopping trips more streamlined and hassle-free.

- **Recognizing the Furry Members of the Family**

Apple's commitment to inclusivity extends beyond the human realm in macOS Sonoma. The Photos app now recognizes pets alongside humans, enabling users to organize and categorize photos of their beloved furry companions easily. This feature taps into people's deep emotional connections with their animal companions, ensuring that cherished memories captured on camera are easily accessible and organized.

- **Typing Reimagined: In-line Suggestions**

Typing on a Mac has never been more intuitive and efficient, thanks to macOS Sonoma's in-line typing suggestions. The operating system intelligently suggests words or phrases as users type, allowing for seamless selection and incorporation into the text. This feature enhances typing speed and reduces the cognitive load associated with text entry, enabling users to focus on their thoughts and ideas rather than the mechanics of typing.

- **Video Conferencing**

In the modern era of remote work and virtual collaboration, macOS Sonoma introduces advanced video conferencing features. From studio lighting adjustments that enhance visual clarity to reactions that enable users to express themselves during virtual meetings, Apple has reimagined the video conferencing experience.

Moreover, sharing screens with customizable presenter overlays empowers users to create engaging and immersive presentations. Whether a remote team meeting or a virtual classroom session, these features elevate engagement and interactivity, fostering a more dynamic and inclusive virtual environment.

- **Verdict**

With macOS Sonoma, Apple has again demonstrated its commitment to innovation and user-centric design. From the captivating visual elements to the productivity-enhancing enhancements, this operating system update delivers a comprehensive and cohesive experience that caters to diverse user needs.

How to Identify Your macOS Version

Keeping track of which version of macOS your Mac is running is crucial for ensuring you have access to the latest features and security updates. Apple continues enhancing and refining the macOS experience with every new release.

- **Getting the Version Details**

The first step is to open the **Apple menu** by clicking the **Apple icon** in the top left corner of your screen. In the dropdown menu that appears, select **"About This Mac."** It will open the System Information window.

Here, you'll find the precise version number and name of the macOS your Mac is currently running. For example, suppose your Mac is on the latest release. In that case, you'll see **"macOS Sonoma"** listed prominently, along with version 14.4.1 below.

- **Reveal Additional Mac Specs**

While this System Information window is open, click the **"Overview"** tab on the top to reveal additional helpful specs about your Mac; this includes the model name, processor type, amount of memory, and start-up disk details.

Knowing these specifics allows you to optimize performance based on your Mac's precise capabilities. It also comes in handy when troubleshooting issues or ensuring software compatibility.

- **System Preferences Shortcut**

If you prefer bypassing the Apple menu, there's a handy shortcut for accessing the same System Information window. Open the System Preferences

macOS Sonoma User's Guide

app (found in the Applications folder or by searching with Spotlight), then click on the top bar section showing your Mac's name.

It reveals the overview panel with the macOS version at the front and center. You can even click the **"Software Update"** button to quickly check for available operating system updates to keep your Mac secure and running optimally.

Setting Up macOS Sonoma

Upgrading to the latest macOS version is an exciting process that brings new features and improvements to your Mac. With macOS Sonoma, Apple has introduced a fresh look and several productivity-enhancing capabilities.

- **Preparing for Installation**

Before you begin, ensure your Mac meets the system requirements for Sonoma. Check for compatible hardware and fully back up your data using Time Machine or a cloud service like iCloud Drive. Having a recent backup gives you peace of mind during the transition.

- **Downloading Sonoma**

To access the latest macOS, open the System Preferences app and click **"Software Update."** Your Mac will check for updates and prompt you to download Sonoma. Alternatively, you can download the installer from Apple's website. Once downloaded, the installer will guide you through the straightforward process.

- **The Seamless Setup Experience**

As the installation begins, you'll be greeted with a welcoming setup assistant that streamlines the process. Follow the on-screen prompts to select your preferred language, migrate your data from a backup or another Mac, and sign in with your Apple ID.

For instance, if upgrading from an older Mac, the setup assistant can securely transfer your

macOS Sonoma User's Guide

documents, applications, and settings, making the transition smooth.

- **Personalizing Your Mac**

Sonoma introduces a refreshed look with new wallpapers and desktop icons. Take a moment to explore the revamped System Settings and customize your Mac to your liking. Adjust the desktop background, menu bar, and dock to reflect your style.

CHAPTER TWO

Start Using Apps

With macOS Sonoma, Apple has introduced new ways to interact with your favorite apps, streamlining your workflow and unlocking new productivity levels.

- **Launching Apps**

Let's explore the various paths that lead you to your desired app to kick things off. The classic method is to head to the **Dock**, that ever-present launchpad for your app arsenal. A simple click on the app's icon will whisk it into action. For those who embrace efficiency, using Spotlight's lightning-fast search is a game-changer. Summon this powerful utility with a quick **Command + Space**, then start typing the app's name to reveal it instantly.

- **App Library**

Sonoma unveils the innovative App Library, a curated gallery that showcases all your installed apps in one centralized location. To access this, click the **App Library icon** in your Dock. Once inside, you'll discover apps neatly organized into categories, making navigating and locating your desired tool a breeze.

- **The Command Keys**

For those who revel in keyboard shortcuts, macOS Sonoma has you covered. Effortlessly switch between apps using the timeless **Command + Tab** combination, quickly cycling through your open app windows. If you know the app's name, a swift **Command + Space** followed by typing the app's moniker will instantly transport you there.

- **Multitasking**

Sonoma's **Stage Manager** is a true multitasking maven, allowing you to juggle multiple app windows on a single display seamlessly. With a simple gesture or keyboard shortcut, you can create customized workspaces tailored to your specific needs and smoothly transition between them.

- **The Contextual Menu**

Right-clicking (or Control-clicking) on an app's icon or window unveils a contextual menu brimming with hidden powers. This menu is a gateway to enhanced customization and control, from launching related apps to accessing app-specific preferences.

With these tools at your disposal, navigating and interacting with apps on macOS Sonoma becomes an intuitive experience.

macOS Sonoma User's Guide

The Menu Bar

The Menu Bar sits elegantly at the top of your Mac's screen, always within reach. It's a sleek, semi-transparent bar that houses app menus, system icons, and the iconic Apple logo. With macOS Sonoma, the Menu Bar has received a subtle visual update, blending seamlessly with the refined aesthetics of the operating system.

- **Accessing the Menu Bar**

There are multiple ways to access the Menu Bar on your Mac running macOS Sonoma:

Mouse or Trackpad: Move your cursor to the top of the screen, and the Menu Bar will appear, revealing its contents.

Keyboard Shortcut: Press the Control + F3 key combination to instantly reveal the Menu Bar, no matter where your cursor is positioned.

Touch Bar (on compatible Macs): If your Mac has a Touch Bar, you can access the Menu Bar by tapping the Menu Bar icon on the Touch Bar. Exploring the Menu Bar

Once the Menu Bar is visible, you'll notice a wealth of information and functionality at your fingertips:

App Menus: Each open app displays its menu in the Menu Bar, providing quick access to its features and settings.

System Icons: The Menu Bar houses various system icons, such as Wi-Fi, Bluetooth, and battery indicators, allowing you to monitor and control these functions with ease.

Spotlight Search: Quickly access it by clicking on the magnifying glass icon, making it easier to find files and apps and perform web searches.

Control Center: With a single click on the Control Center icon, you can access various system controls and settings, including display brightness, volume, and more.

Customization Options: Right-click on the Menu Bar to customize its appearance and behavior, such as hiding or rearranging icons or enabling the battery percentage display.

The Dock

The Dock is a sleek, translucent bar at the bottom of your Mac's screen by default, though you can reposition it to the left or right side if desired. It's home to app icons, file and folder shortcuts, and open windows, allowing you to navigate your Mac easily. In macOS Sonoma, the Dock has received a visual refresh, with subtle design tweaks that enhance its integration with the aesthetic of the operating system.

- **Accessing the Dock**

Accessing the Dock is as simple as moving your cursor to the screen's bottom (or side), where it will automatically appear. However, macOS Sonoma introduces a new, quicker way to summon the Dock:

Keyboard Shortcut: Press the Control + Option + D key combination to instantly reveal the Dock, no matter where your cursor is positioned on the screen.

Mouse or Trackpad: Move your cursor to the screen's bottom (or side), and the Dock will appear, just like in previous macOS versions. Exploring the Dock

Once the Dock is visible, you'll notice its intuitive layout and features:

App Icons: Launch your favorite apps by clicking on their icons in the Dock.

Open Windows: Any open windows or files will appear as separate icons in the Dock, allowing you to switch between them with a single click.

Recent and Frequently Used Apps: The Dock automatically displays recently opened and frequently used apps, making accessing the apps you use most efficient.

Customization Options: Right-click on the Dock to customize its appearance and behavior, such as adjusting the size and magnification or enabling automatic hide and show.

Dock Folders: Group related apps or files together by creating Dock folders, decluttering your Dock and improving organization.

- **Using the Dock Effectively**

The Dock is designed to simplify your workflow and enhance productivity. Here are some tips to make the most of this powerful feature:

Drag and Drop: Easily move files or folders to the Dock by dragging and dropping them onto an app icon and opening the associated app with the dropped item(s).

Quick Actions: Press and hold the Control key while clicking an app icon to reveal quick actions, such as opening a new window or accessing recent documents.

Dock Stacking: Group related app windows together by clicking and holding on an app icon, then selecting the desired window from the stacked icons.

The Finder

The Finder is the ever-present file manager in macOS, visually representing your Mac's file structure. It's a handy tool that allows you to create, copy, move, and delete files and folders and access various system locations and external storage devices. In macOS Sonoma, the Finder has received a visual overhaul, with a cleaner and more modern interface that blends seamlessly with the operating system's aesthetic.

- **Accessing the Finder**

There are multiple ways to access the Finder on your Mac running macOS Sonoma:

macOS Sonoma User's Guide

Dock: Click on the Finder icon in the Dock, which resembles a smiling face, to launch the Finder.

Keyboard Shortcut: Press Command + N to open a new Finder window instantly.

Spotlight Search: Use Spotlight Search to find and open the Finder by typing "Finder" in the search field.

Menu Bar: Navigate to the Go menu in the Menu Bar, and select the "Finder" option to open the Finder.

- **Exploring the Finder**

Once the Finder is open, you'll be greeted by a familiar yet refined interface:

Sidebar: The Sidebar provides quick access to frequently used locations, such as Desktop, Documents, Downloads, and external storage devices. You can customize the Sidebar to display your preferred locations.

Preview Pane: The Preview Pane allows you to preview the contents of a selected file without opening it, saving time and providing a quick glimpse of your files.

Toolbar: The Toolbar offers a range of actions and tools, such as creating new folders, accessing search, and sharing options.

View Options: Adjust how your files and folders are displayed by choosing from various options, including Icon, List, Column, and Gallery views.

Quick Actions: A contextual menu with 'Quick Actions' will open when you right-click a file or folder, enabling you to perform everyday tasks like opening, sharing, or compressing files with a few clicks.

Spotlight

Spotlight is a ubiquitous feature in macOS, accessible from anywhere on your Mac's desktop. It's a lightning-fast search engine that scans your entire file system, applications, and even the internet, delivering relevant results in an instant.

- **Accessing Spotlight**

There are multiple ways to access Spotlight on your Mac running macOS Sonoma:

Keyboard Shortcut: Press the Command + Space bar to instantly summon the Spotlight search field, no matter what application or window you're currently in.

Menu Bar: Click on the magnifying glass icon in the Menu Bar to open the Spotlight search field.

Spotlight Window: Navigate to the Spotlight icon in the Dock or use Spotlight Search to find and open the Spotlight window.

Siri: Ask Siri to search for specific items or information using natural language commands, and Spotlight will provide the results.

Once Spotlight is open, you'll notice its intuitive interface and powerful search capabilities:

Search Field: Type your search query into the Spotlight search field, and it will instantly start displaying relevant results.

Result Categories: Spotlight organizes search results into categories, such as Applications, Documents, Web Searches, and more, making it easier to find what you're looking for.

Preview and Quick Actions: Hover over a search result to preview its contents or access Quick Actions, allowing you to perform everyday tasks without opening the item itself.

Spotlight Suggestions: As you type, Spotlight will suggest relevant options based on your search query, helping you refine your search and find what you need faster.

Search Scope: Customize the scope to include or exclude specific locations, file types, or metadata, ensuring that Spotlight searches precisely where you want it to.

- **Using Spotlight Effectively**

Spotlight is designed to save you time and streamline your workflow. Here are some tips to make the most of this powerful feature:

Advanced Queries: Use advanced search operators like "kind:" or "date:" to narrow your search results by file type or creation/modification date.

Calculations and Conversions: Spotlight can perform simple calculations and unit conversions, making it a handy tool for quick math and measurement tasks.

System Preferences: Search for specific system settings or preferences directly in Spotlight; you can access and adjust them instantly.

Using Your Mouse or Trackpad

The mouse is a handheld pointing device that allows you to control the cursor on your Mac's screen. At the same time, the trackpad is a touch-sensitive surface integrated into most modern Mac laptops and some desktop keyboards. Both devices provide a seamless and natural way to interact with your Mac, enabling you to navigate, select, and perform various actions efficiently.

- **Basic Mouse and Trackpad Gestures**

Before diving into the advanced features, let's cover the basic gestures for using the mouse and trackpad:

Pointer Movement: Move the mouse or slide your finger across the trackpad to control the cursor's position on the screen.

Clicking: Press the mouse button or tap the trackpad with one finger to select or activate an item.

Right-clicking: Press the right mouse button or tap the trackpad with two fingers to access contextual menus or perform secondary actions.

macOS Sonoma User's Guide

Scrolling: Use the scroll wheel on your mouse or perform a two-finger swipe gesture on the trackpad to scroll through content vertically or horizontally.

- **Advanced Features**

macOS Sonoma introduces several new features and enhancements to the mouse and trackpad experience:

Force Touch (Trackpad Only): Apply varying pressure levels on the trackpad to perform different actions, such as previewing files, accessing contextual menus, or activating Force Touch shortcuts.

Gestures and Shortcuts: Configure customizable gestures and shortcuts for the mouse or trackpad to streamline your workflow; this includes pinching to zoom, swiping between spaces or full-screen apps, or activating Mission Control with a specific gesture.

Accessibility Features: macOS Sonoma offers a range of accessibility features for the mouse and trackpad, including adjustable pointer size, cursor customization, and pointer tracking enhancements for improved visibility and precision.

Multi-Touch Gestures (Trackpad Only): Perform advanced multi-touch gestures on the trackpad, such as swiping with three or four fingers to switch between open apps or activate Mission Control, respectively.

- **Customizing Your Experience**

One of the great strengths of macOS Sonoma is the ability to customize your mouse and trackpad experience to suit your personal preferences and workflow:

Tracking Speed: Adjust the tracking speed of your mouse or trackpad to find the perfect balance between precision and responsiveness.

Scrolling Behavior: Customize the scrolling behavior, such as turning inertia scrolling on or off, reverse scrolling direction, or adjusting scroll speed.

Button Remapping: Remap the functionality of mouse buttons or trackpad gestures to perform different actions or shortcuts.

Using the Keyboard

The keyboard is a fundamental tool for inputting text, navigating interfaces, and executing various commands on your Mac. With its combination of alphanumeric, function, and specialized keys like the Command, Option, and Control keys, the keyboard provides a versatile and efficient way to interact with your Mac.

- **Accessing Keyboard Settings**

To customize and optimize your keyboard experience, you'll need to access the keyboard settings in macOS Sonoma:

System Preferences: Click on the Apple menu in the top-left corner of your screen, then select "System Preferences." In the System Preferences window, click the "Keyboard" icon to access the keyboard settings.

Spotlight Search: Press the Command + Space bar to open Spotlight Search, then type "Keyboard" and select the "Keyboard" preference pane from the results.

- **Exploring Keyboard Settings**

Once you've accessed the keyboard settings, you'll discover a wealth of customization options and features:

Key Repeat and Delay Until Repeat: Adjust the rate at which keys repeat when held down and the delay before the repetition starts, allowing you to find the perfect balance between responsiveness and accuracy.

Text Substitutions and Dictionaries: Create custom text substitutions and add dictionaries to enable automatic word replacements or expansions, saving you time and effort when typing (frequently) used phrases or words.

Keyboard Shortcuts: Customize keyboard shortcuts for various actions and applications, streamlining your workflow by assigning frequently used commands to easily accessible vital combinations.

Input Sources: Add and switch between different keyboard layouts, languages, and input methods, making it easy to type in multiple languages or use specialized character sets.

Dictation and Voice Control: Enable dictation and voice control features, allowing you to input text and control your Mac using voice commands for a hands-free experience.

Taking Screenshots

Screenshots represent your Mac's screen or a selected portion captured as an image file. They can be beneficial for various purposes, such as documenting errors, illustrating software usage, or sharing information visually. MacOS Sonoma offers multiple ways to take screenshots, each with its options and customizations.

- **Accessing the Screenshot Feature**

There are several methods to access and take screenshots on your Mac running macOS Sonoma:

Keyboard Shortcuts: Use predefined keyboard shortcuts to capture the entire screen, a selected area, or a specific window.

Screenshot Toolbar: Activate the Screenshot toolbar from the menu bar or through a keyboard shortcut to access advanced screenshot options.

Preview App: Open the Preview app and use its built-in screenshot capabilities to capture images.

Screenshot Settings: Customize the screenshot experience by accessing the screenshot settings in the System Preferences.

macOS Sonoma User's Guide

- **Taking Screenshots**

Once you've accessed the screenshot feature, you'll discover a variety of options and tools to capture your screen:

Capture Entire Screen: Press Command + Shift + 3 to capture the entire screen as an image file.

Capture Selected Area: Press Command + Shift + 4, then drag your cursor to select the desired area to capture.

Capture a Window: Press Command + Shift + 4, press the Space bar and click on the window you want to capture.

Screenshot Toolbar: The Screenshot toolbar can access advanced options like delayed capture, recording video, and more.

Screenshot Settings: Customize your screenshots' default save location, file format, and other preferences.

- **Working with Screenshots**

After taking a screenshot, you'll have several options for managing and editing the captured image:

Preview App: Open the Preview app to view, annotate, and edit screenshots using tools like markup, shapes, and text.

Sharing Options: Share your screenshots directly from the Preview app or the Screenshot toolbar by clicking the Share button and choosing your preferred sharing method.

Screenshot Editor: macOS Sonoma introduces a new built-in screenshot editor, allowing you to make quick edits and annotations without opening a separate app.

CHAPTER THREE

Working with Windows

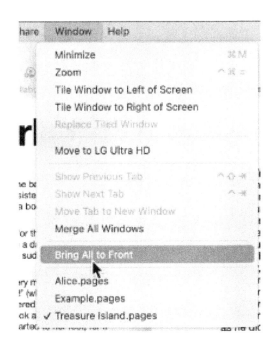

The Window tab is a tool that allows you to organize and manage multiple windows within a single application. Imagine having all your web pages, documents, or media files neatly arranged in a tabbed interface, eliminating the need for cluttered desktops or excessive window switching. You can effortlessly navigate between open items with a few simple clicks, streamlining your multitasking capabilities.

- **Accessing the Window Tab**

macOS Sonoma offers several intuitive ways to access and utilize the Window Tab feature:

Menu Bar: Look for the "Window" menu in your application. Within this menu, you'll find options to merge all windows into a single tabbed window or create a new one.

Keyboard Shortcuts: Take advantage of keyboard shortcuts for a more efficient approach. Press "Command + T" to open a new tab within the current window or "Command + Shift +]" to move to the next tab.

Drag and Drop: Embrace the tactile experience by dragging one window onto another. This action will automatically merge the two windows into a single tabbed interface.

Imagine you're working on a research project with multiple web pages and documents open

macOS Sonoma User's Guide

simultaneously. Instead of constantly switching between windows, you can merge them into a single tabbed window, allowing you to easily navigate and reference different sources without losing focus.

Customizing Window Tab Settings

While the default settings provide a solid foundation, macOS Sonoma allows you to tailor the Window Tab experience to your needs. Access the **"System Preferences"** and navigate to the **"Window Tab"** panel to explore various customization options:

Appearance: Adjust the visual style of your tabs, including color, size, and position within the window.

Behavior: Determine how tabs behave when opened, closed, or rearranged. You can also turn on or off specific actions, such as tab previews or automatic tab switching.

Keyboard Shortcuts: Customize keyboard shortcuts for everyday tab-related actions, ensuring a seamless and efficient workflow tailored to your preferences.

Opening and Closing Apps

Launching applications on your Mac is a breeze, with multiple options at your disposal:

Dock: The Dock is a handy tool that provides quick access to frequently used apps. Click on the desired app icon to launch it.

Launchpad: Pinching with your thumb and three fingers on the trackpad or clicking the Launchpad icon in the Dock displays all your installed apps in a visually appealing grid layout.

Spotlight Search: Invoke Spotlight by pressing "Command + Space" and typing the app's name. Spotlight will intelligently suggest matching applications, allowing you to launch them with a simple click or keyboard shortcut.

Finder: Navigate to the "Applications" folder in Finder, locate the desired app, and double-click to open it.

Imagine you're a graphic designer eager to dive into your latest project. With a simple click on the Adobe Photoshop icon in the Dock or a quick Spotlight search, you can instantly launch the app and immerse yourself in your creative endeavors.

Closing Apps on macOS Sonoma

Jusl as opening apps is essential, properly closing them when you're done is equally important. macOS Sonoma offers several intuitive methods to quit applications:

Menu Bar: Look for the app's name in the menu bar and select "Quit" from the dropdown menu.

Keyboard Shortcut: Press "Command + Q" to quit the active app quickly.

Window Controls: Click the red "close" button in the top-left corner of the app window to close it.

Force Quit: If an app becomes unresponsive, you can force quit it by pressing "Command + Option + Esc" and selecting the problematic app from the list.

Customizing App Settings

macOS Sonoma empowers you to tailor app settings to your preferences. Access the **"System Preferences"** and explore the various options available for each app. You can adjust settings for notifications, keyboard shortcuts, file associations, and more, ensuring a personalized and efficient experience.

Finding Apps

macOS Sonoma introduces the revolutionary App Library, a centralized hub that is a one-stop shop for all your applications. With a simple click or swipe, you can access a visually appealing grid of app icons organized intelligently into categories based on their functionality. This streamlined approach makes it easier to locate the app you need, whether it's a productivity tool, a creative suite, or an entertainment platform.

- **The Power of Spotlight**

Spotlight, macOS's built-in search engine, is a versatile tool that can be leveraged to find apps with lightning speed. Press "**Command + Space**" to summon the Spotlight interface, and start typing the name of the app you're looking for. Spotlight will instantly display relevant results, including installed apps, web searches, and even suggestions for apps available in the App Store.

Instead of sifting through countless folders or scrolling endlessly through the App Library, a simple Spotlight search will instantly surface the app you need, allowing you to launch it with a single click or keystroke.

- **App Settings**

Once you've located and launched your desired app, macOS Sonoma empowers you to tailor its settings to your needs. Access the **"System Preferences"** and navigate to the appropriate panel for the app. Here, you can adjust various settings, including keyboard shortcuts, file associations, notifications, and more, ensuring a personalized experience that aligns with your unique workflow.

- **Embracing the App Store**

You can browse through curated collections, read reviews, and seamlessly install or update apps directly from the App Store. This centralized platform ensures you always have access to the

macOS Sonoma User's Guide

latest and greatest software offerings, keeping your Mac up-to-date and performing at its best.

Installing and Uninstalling Apps

macOS Sonoma offers a variety of methods to acquire and install new applications, catering to different preferences and requirements:

App Store: The App Store is a one-stop shop for discovering and installing various apps, ranging from productivity tools to creative suites. With a few clicks, you can browse, purchase, and install apps directly from the App Store, ensuring a seamless and secure experience.

Direct Download: Many developers can download apps directly from their websites. After downloading the app package, double-click to initiate the installation process.

Disk Image (.dmg) Files: Some apps are distributed as disk image files. Mount the disk image, and drag the app icon to the "Applications" folder to install it.

Installer Packages (.pkg): Certain apps come bundled as installer packages. Double-click the package file and follow the on-screen instructions to complete the installation.

Suppose you're a graphic designer needing a powerful image editing tool. With a quick search in the App Store, you can quickly locate and install the latest version of your preferred software, ensuring you have the right tools to bring your creative visions to life.

Uninstalling Apps on macOS Sonoma

Just as installing apps is essential, removing unwanted or outdated applications is equally important for maintaining a clutter-free and efficient system. macOS Sonoma offers several methods to uninstall apps:

macOS Sonoma User's Guide

Launchpad: In the Launchpad, locate the app you wish to uninstall and click the "Options" button (represented by an ellipsis). Select "Delete" to remove the app from your Mac.

Finder: Open the "Applications" folder in Finder, locate the app you want to uninstall and drag it to the Trash. Alternatively, right-click the app and select "Move to Trash."

App Uninstallers: Some apps come bundled with their uninstaller utility, which can be found within the app or in the "Applications" folder. Follow the prompts to remove the app and any associated files safely.

Customizing App Settings

Once you've installed your desired apps, macOS Sonoma empowers you to tailor their settings to your preferences. Access the **"System Preferences"** and navigate to the appropriate panel for the app. Here, you can adjust various settings, including keyboard shortcuts, file associations, notifications, and more, ensuring a personalized experience that aligns with your unique workflow.

Organizing Apps in The Dock and Launchpad

The Dock tool is a convenient launchpad for your most frequently used applications. With a few simple steps, you can curate the Dock to showcase your essential apps, keeping them easily accessible and visually appealing:

Adding Apps to the Dock: Locate the app you wish to add in the Finder or Launchpad and drag and drop its icon onto the Dock. Alternatively, you can right-click on the app and select "Options > Keep in Dock."

Rearranging Apps: To reorganize the apps in the Dock, click and hold on an app icon, then drag it to the desired position.

Removing Apps from the Dock: Right-click on the app icon you wish to remove and select "Options >

Remove from Dock." Alternatively, you can drag the icon from the Dock to remove it.

Imagine you're a creative professional juggling multiple design tools. By organizing your most-used apps like Adobe Photoshop, Illustrator, and InDesign in the Dock, you can seamlessly switch between them, streamlining your creative workflow and boosting productivity.

- **The Launchpad**

The Launchpad features a comprehensive overview of all your installed applications, organized in a visually appealing grid layout. With a few simple gestures or clicks, you can access and arrange your apps with ease:

Accessing the Launchpad: Pinch with your thumb and three fingers on the trackpad or click the Launchpad icon in the Dock to reveal the Launchpad interface.

Organizing Apps: Within the Launchpad, you can drag and drop apps to reorder them or create custom app folders by dragging one app icon onto another.

Removing Apps: To remove an app from the Launchpad, click and hold on its icon until it starts to jiggle, then click the "X" button that appears.

Customizing App Settings

macOS Sonoma empowers you to tailor the appearance and behavior of your Dock and Launchpad to suit your personal preferences. Access the "System Preferences" and navigate to the respective panels to explore a range of customization options:

Dock Settings: Adjust the Dock's position, size, magnification, and animations. You can also turn features like auto-hide and recent app indicators on or off.

Launchpad Settings: Customize the Launchpad's grid layout, icon size, and app sorting options. You

macOS Sonoma User's Guide

can also choose to display or hide recently downloaded apps.

CHAPTER FOUR

Navigating the Finder Window and Toolbar

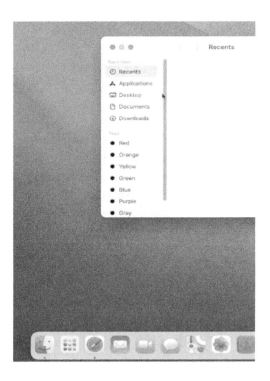

The Finder window and toolbar are integral to the macOS Sonoma experience, providing a user-friendly interface for navigating your files and folders.

macOS Sonoma User's Guide

Accessing the Finder Window

The Finder window is your gateway to the macOS file system. You can access it in several ways:

Dock: Click on the smiley face icon in the Dock to open a new Finder window.

Keyboard Shortcut: Press Command + N to launch a new Finder instance.

Spotlight Search: Use the Spotlight Search functionality (Command + Space bar) and type "Finder" to open the application.

Exploring the Finder Window

Once the Finder window opens, you'll be greeted with a clean, intuitive interface. The Sidebar on the left side provides quick access to frequently used locations, such as your Desktop, Documents, and iCloud Drive folders.

The main area, the Browser, displays the contents of the currently selected location. You can navigate through folders, preview files, and perform various actions like copying, moving, or deleting items.

Customizing the Toolbar

The Finder toolbar at the top of the window offers many tools and shortcuts to streamline your workflow. By default, it displays essential functions like creating a new Folder, getting info about a selected item, and sharing files. However, you can customize the toolbar to suit your specific needs.

To add or remove toolbar items, simply **Control-click (or right-click)** on the toolbar and select **"Customize Toolbar..."** from the contextual menu. A sheet will appear, allowing you to drag and drop desired items onto the toolbar. This personalization ensures that your most frequently used tools are always within easy reach.

macOS Sonoma User's Guide

- **Leveraging the Preview Pane**

The Preview Pane is a handy feature that provides a quick glimpse of a file's contents without opening it. To enable the Preview Pane, navigate to the **Finder menu** and select **"View" > "Show Preview."** Alternatively, you can use the keyboard shortcut **(Shift + Command + P)**.

With the Preview Pane enabled, you can select any file in the Browser, and its contents will be displayed in the pane on the right side of the window. This feature is handy for quickly viewing documents, images, or even video and audio files without opening them in their respective applications.

- **Quick Look**

Quick Look is a macOS feature that allows you to preview files without opening them fully. To use Quick Look, select a file in the Finder and press the Space bar. A full-screen preview of the file will appear, complete with navigation controls and essential editing tools for specific file types.

Quick Look is beneficial for quickly viewing and annotating documents, images, and even video and audio files without the overhead of launching their respective applications.

Using the Search Function to Locate Files

The Finder search function is remarkably intuitive and flexible. To perform a basic search, type the name (or part of the name) of the file or folder you're looking for into the search field. As you type, the Finder will dynamically update the results, displaying all matching items in real-time.

For example, if you're looking for a document called "Annual Report 2023," simply type "Annual

Report" into the search field, and the Finder will display all files and folders containing those words in their names.

- **Advanced Search Operators**

While basic searches are powerful, macOS Sonoma's Finder search offers a suite of advanced operators that can help you refine your search and zero in on specific items more efficiently. Here are a few examples:

Kind: To search for a specific file type, use the "kind:" operator followed by the file extension or type (e.g., "kind:pdf" or "kind:image").

Date: To find files modified, created, or last opened within a specific date range, use the "date:" operator followed by the desired time frame (e.g., "date:today" or "date:last week").

Size: To search for files based on their size, use the "size:" operator followed by the desired file size range (e.g., "size:>10MB" or "size:<1GB").

Content: To search within the content of files (e.g., text documents, PDFs, etc.), use the "contents:" operator followed by the desired keyword or phrase (e.g., "contents:'financial report'").

You can combine multiple operators to create particular searches, such as "kind:pdf date:last month size:>5MB," to find large PDF files modified within the last month.

- **Saving and Reusing Searches**

One of the most powerful features of the Finder search is the ability to save and reuse searches you frequently need to find a particular type of file or document. Instead of manually entering the same search criteria each time, you can save the search as a Smart Folder.

To create a Smart Folder, perform your desired search, then choose **"File" > "Save Search"** from the Finder menu. Give your search a name, and it will appear in the Sidebar for easy access in the future.

Viewing and Customizing the Path Bar

Navigating through the intricate file system on your Mac can be a daunting task, especially when you find yourself buried deep within a labyrinth of folders. The Finder offers a handy tool called the Path Bar, which visually represents your current location and allows you to traverse the folder hierarchy with a few clicks effortlessly.

- **Enabling the Path Bar**

Before taking advantage of the Path Bar, you must ensure it's visible in the Finder window. Here's how:

Open a Finder window by clicking on the smiley face icon in the Dock or using the keyboard shortcut (Command + N).

From the **Finder** menu, select **"View" > "Show Path Bar"** or press the Option + Command + P keyboard shortcut.

The Path Bar will now appear at the bottom of the Finder window, displaying the complete path to your current location.

Understanding the Path Bar

The Path Bar visualizes the folder hierarchy, with each level represented by a separate segment. The rightmost segment displays the current folder or location. In contrast, the segments to the left represent the parent folders leading up to that location.

For example, suppose you're viewing the contents of a folder named **"Documents"** in the **"User"** folder. In that case, the Path Bar might display: **"Macintosh HD > Users > Your_Username > Documents"**.

- **Navigating with the Path Bar**

One of the primary benefits of the Path Bar is its ability to facilitate seamless navigation through the folder structure. Instead of repeatedly clicking through multiple levels of folders, you can click on any segment in the Path Bar to instantly jump to that location.

This functionality is convenient when quickly moving between deeply nested folders or revisiting a previously accessed location.

- **Customizing the Path Bar**

While the Path Bar is a valuable tool for navigation, its default appearance might not suit everyone's preferences. Fortunately, macOS Sonoma allows you to customize the Path Bar to better align with your workflow and visual preferences.

To customize the Path Bar, follow these steps:

Open a Finder window and ensure the Path Bar is visible. Control-click (or right-click) on the Path Bar and select **"Show Path Bar Options"** from the contextual menu. In the dialog box that appears, you can choose different options to tailor the Path Bar's appearance and behavior.

Some customization options include:

Displaying the full path or just the last few segments

Showing or hiding the desktop icon

Turning on or off the Path Bar's text ellipsis

Adjusting the Path Bar's font size and color

Customize the Path Bar to suit your preferences, and embrace its potential to enhance your productivity and organizational skills on your Mac.

Adding Application, File, and Folder Shortcuts to the Toolbar

The Finder Toolbar is a customizable area at the top of every Finder window. It displays commonly used buttons and icons by default, such as creating new folders, getting file information, and sharing items. However, the true power of the Toolbar lies in its ability to be tailored to your specific needs by adding shortcuts to your most frequently accessed applications, files, and folders.

- ## Adding Application Shortcuts to the Toolbar

Imagine launching your favorite applications right from the Finder window with a single click. Here's how to add application shortcuts to the Toolbar:

Open a **Finder window** and locate the application you want to add in the Applications folder or by using Spotlight Search. Drag and drop the application icon onto the Toolbar.

A small green plus sign will appear, indicating that the application shortcut is ready to be added. Release the mouse button, and the application icon will now be visible in the Toolbar.

Repeat these steps for each application you want quick access to, and you'll have a personalized Toolbar that can significantly streamline your workflow.

Adding File and Folder Shortcuts to the Toolbar

In addition to application shortcuts, the Finder Toolbar can also be populated with shortcuts to your frequently accessed files and folders. This feature suits those who regularly work with specific documents or projects. Here's how to add file and folder shortcuts:

Open a Finder window and navigate to the file or folder you want to add.

Drag and drop the item onto the Toolbar. As with applications, a small green plus sign will appear, indicating that the shortcut is ready to be added. Release the mouse button, and the file or folder icon will now be visible in the Toolbar.

By having your most important files and folders just a click away, you'll save time and effort that would otherwise be spent navigating through multiple levels of folders or using search functions.

- **Customizing the Toolbar**

While adding shortcuts is a great way to streamline your workflow, macOS Sonoma's Finder Toolbar offers even more customization options. To access these options, simply Control-click (or right-click) on the Toolbar and select **"Customize Toolbar..."** from the contextual menu.

A sheet will appear, displaying all the available Toolbar items. You can drag and drop items to rearrange their order or remove them entirely from the Toolbar. This level of customization ensures that your Toolbar remains clutter-free and focused on the tools and shortcuts you genuinely need.

Customizing the Finder Toolbar for Quick Access

Before you can customize the Finder Toolbar, you'll need to ensure it's visible in your Finder windows. Here's how:

Open a Finder window by clicking on the smiley face icon in the Dock or using the keyboard shortcut (Command + N).

From the Finder menu, select **"View" > "Show Toolbar"** or press the Option + Command + T keyboard shortcut.

The Finder Toolbar will now appear at the top of the Finder window, ready for you to unleash its full potential.

- **Customizing the Toolbar**

With the Finder Toolbar visible, it's time to tailor it to your needs. Follow these steps to customize the toolbar:

Control-click (or right-click) on the Toolbar and select **"Customize Toolbar..."** from the contextual menu.

A sheet will appear, displaying all the available toolbar items.

macOS Sonoma User's Guide

To add an item, drag and drop it from the sheet onto the Toolbar.

To remove an item, drag it off the Toolbar and back onto the sheet.

Rearrange the order of items by dragging and dropping them into your desired positions.

- **Toolbar Item Options**

The Finder Toolbar offers various customization options, allowing you to add shortcuts for applications, files, folders, and even specialized tools. Here are some of the most valuable items you can add to your Toolbar:

Applications: Quickly launch your favorite apps with a single click.

Files and Folders: Add shortcuts to frequently accessed documents, projects, or locations.

Path Buttons: Navigate your file system easily using the hierarchical path buttons.

Quick Look: Preview files without opening them by adding the Quick Look button.

Share Menu: Share files effortlessly with the Share Menu button.

Tags: Access and manage your file tags with the dedicated Tags button.

- **Creating Custom Toolbar Items**

While the default toolbar items cover many functions, macOS Sonoma takes customization further by allowing you to create custom toolbar items. These can be shortcuts to specific folders, applications, or AppleScript scripts.

To create a custom toolbar item, follow these steps:

Locate the item you want to add (e.g., a folder, application, or script).

Drag and drop the item onto the Finder Toolbar.

A green plus sign will appear, indicating the item is ready to be added.

Release the mouse button, and the custom item will now be visible in the Toolbar.

Utilizing the Preview Pane for Quick File Viewing

Before using the Preview Pane, you'll need to ensure it's visible in your Finder windows. Here's how:

Open a Finder window by clicking on the smiley face icon in the Dock or using the keyboard shortcut (Command + N).

From the Finder menu, select **"View" > "Show Preview"** or press the Shift + Command + P keyboard shortcut.

The Preview Pane will now appear on the right side of the Finder window, ready to display the contents of any selected file.

- **Previewing Files**

With the Preview Pane enabled you can effortlessly preview a wide range of file types without opening them in their respective applications. Please select a file in the Finder window; its contents will instantly be displayed in the Preview Pane.

For text-based documents, such as Word files, PDFs, or plain text files, you'll see a clear and legible preview of the document's contents, complete with formatting and layout. This feature is advantageous for quickly scanning through documents without the need to open them fully.

The Preview Pane also helps with multimedia files. Select an image file, and you'll see a high-quality preview of the image, allowing you to inspect its details without launching an image editing application. Similarly, you can preview video and audio files, complete with playback controls, making it easy to review their contents quickly.

macOS Sonoma User's Guide

- **Navigating and Customizing the Preview Pane**

The Preview Pane offers a range of navigational and customization options to enhance your file preview experience. You can use the scroll bar or arrow keys to navigate the content for longer documents or image sequences. Additionally, you can adjust the zoom level or rotate images directly within the Preview Pane, eliminating the need to open them in a separate application.

The Preview Pane also supports Quick Look, macOS's built-in file preview tool, for added convenience. Pressing the Space bar while a file is selected allows you to enter Quick Look mode, which provides a full-screen preview and additional editing tools for specific file types.

- **Optimizing the Preview Pane**

To make the most of the Preview Pane, you can customize its appearance and behavior to suit your preferences. Control-click (or right-click) on the

Preview Pane and select **"Preview Options"** to access various settings.

In the Preview Pane, you can display file information from this menu, such as size and creation date. You can adjust the font size and style for text previews, ensuring optimal readability.

Exploring the Sidebar for Favorite Locations and Tags

The Sidebar is a prominent feature in every Finder window, located on the left side of the interface. If it's not visible in your current Finder window, you can easily enable it by following these steps:

Open a Finder window by clicking on the smiley face icon in the Dock or using the keyboard shortcut (Command + N).

From the Finder menu, select **"View" > "Show Sidebar"** or press the Option + Command + S keyboard shortcut.

macOS Sonoma User's Guide

The Sidebar will now appear, revealing a wealth of organizational tools and shortcuts.

- **Favorite Locations**

One of the primary functions of the Sidebar is to provide quick access to your frequently visited locations. It includes shortcuts to your Desktop, Documents, Downloads, and other commonly used folders by default. However, you can customize this section by adding your favorite locations.

Drag and drop the folder from the Finder window onto the Favourites section to add a folder to the Sidebar's Favorites section. This action creates a shortcut, allowing you to quickly navigate to that location with a single click, saving you valuable time and effort.

- **Exploring and Utilizing Tags**

In addition to favorite locations, the Sidebar offers a robust tagging system that can revolutionize how you organize your files and folders. macOS

Sonoma's tagging feature allows you to assign colorful, descriptive labels to your items, making it easier to categorize and locate them later.

To access the Tags section in the Sidebar, click the **"Tags"** header. You'll find a list of all the tags you've created and their corresponding colors here. Clicking on a specific tag will display all the files and folders assigned to it, regardless of their location on your Mac.

You can create new tags by clicking on the **"+"** **button** at the bottom of the Tags section or by right-clicking (or Control-clicking) on a file or folder and selecting **"Tags..."** from the contextual menu.

- **Customizing the Sidebar**

While the Sidebar offers a wealth of organizational tools, macOS Sonoma allows you to customize it further to suit your needs. Control-clicking (or right-clicking) on the Sidebar will enable you to access various options to show or hide different sections, such as Recent Locations, iCloud, and connected servers or external drives.

Additionally, you can rearrange the order of the sections by simply dragging and dropping them within the Sidebar. This level of customization ensures that your Sidebar remains streamlined and focused on the tools and locations most relevant to your workflow.

Syncing Files and Data Between Mac and Other Devices

macOS Sonoma's Finder offers seamless syncing capabilities that perfectly harmonise your files and data across your Mac, iPhone, iPad, and other computers.

- **Syncing with iCloud**

One of the most convenient ways to sync your files and data between your Mac and other devices is through iCloud, Apple's cloud storage service. By enabling iCloud on your devices, you can access and manage your documents, photos, notes, and more from anywhere with an internet connection.

To get started with iCloud syncing:

Open System Preferences on your Mac and click the **"Apple ID"** icon.

Ensure your Apple ID is signed in and select the **"iCloud"** option.

Choose which apps and services you want to sync with iCloud, such as iCloud Drive, Photos, Notes, and more.

With iCloud syncing enabled, any changes or additions you make to your files and data on your Mac will automatically sync across your other devices connected to the same iCloud account.

- **Utilizing iCloud Drive**

iCloud Drive is a powerful feature within iCloud that allows you to store and access your files and folders directly from the Finder on your Mac. By saving your documents and projects to iCloud Drive, you can ensure they're always up-to-date and available on all your devices.

To access iCloud Drive from the Finder:

Open a Finder window and click the **"iCloud Drive"** option in the Sidebar.

Here, you can create new folders, upload files, and manage your cloud-based data just as you would with local files and folders.

Any changes you make to files and folders within iCloud Drive will automatically sync across your devices, ensuring you always have the latest versions at your fingertips.

- **Syncing with Third-Party Cloud Services**

While iCloud provides seamless integration with Apple devices, macOS Sonoma also supports syncing with popular third-party cloud storage services like Dropbox, Google Drive, and Microsoft OneDrive. These services offer additional storage options and can be particularly useful if you frequently collaborate with others or work across different platforms.

To sync with a third-party cloud service:

Open the respective cloud storage app or sign in through your web browser.

Follow the prompts to set up syncing between your Mac and the cloud service.

Choose which folders or files you want to sync; the service will handle the rest.

With these third-party cloud services, you can access your files and data from any device with an internet connection, ensuring you're always up-to-date and in sync.

Keyboard Shortcuts for Efficient Finder Usage

Before diving into the shortcuts, let's start with the basics: opening a Finder window. Instead of navigating through menus or clicking on icons, you can instantly summon a new Finder window using the following keyboard shortcut:

- **Command + N**

This shortcut will open a fresh Finder window, allowing you to explore and manage your files and folders.

- **Navigating the Finder**

Once you have a Finder window open, you can use a variety of keyboard shortcuts to navigate through your file system with ease. Here are some essential shortcuts to get you started:

Command + Up Arrow: Move up onc level in the folder hierarchy

Command + Down Arrow: Move down one level into the selected folder

Command + Shift + G: Open the "Go to Folder" dialog, allowing you to jump to a specific location quickly

Command + Shift + H: Navigate directly to your home folder

These shortcuts eliminate excessive clicking and scrolling, allowing you to move through your files and folders quickly.

Managing Files and Folders

The Finder offers a wide range of keyboard shortcuts for managing your files and folders, from creating new items to renaming and deleting existing ones. Here are some essential shortcuts to streamline your file management:

Command + Shift + N: Create a new folder in the current location

Command + Delete: Move the selected items to the Trash

Return (or Enter): Rename the selected file or folder

Command + C: Copy the selected items

Command + V: Paste the copied items to the current location

By incorporating these shortcuts into your workflow, you can perform everyday file management tasks remarkably efficiently, saving you valuable time and effort.

Utilizing Finder Window Shortcuts

In addition to navigating and managing files, macOS Sonoma's Finder offers a plethora of keyboard shortcuts for controlling the Finder window itself. These shortcuts can help you customize your workspace and access advanced features with ease:

Command + Option + P: Show or hide the Preview Pane

Command + Option + S: Show or hide the Sidebar

Command + Option + T: Show or hide the Toolbar

Command + Option + F: Search for files and folders using the Spotlight search field

When you master these shortcuts, you can tailor the Finder window to suit your needs, ensuring that your workspace remains clutter-free and focused on the tasks.

Finder Preferences and Settings

To access the Finder's preferences and settings, follow these simple steps:

Open a Finder window by clicking on the smiley face icon in the Dock or using the keyboard shortcut (Command + N).

Select **"Preferences..."** from the Finder menu or use the keyboard shortcut (**Command +,**).

The Finder Preferences window will appear, revealing many options for customizing various aspects of the Finder's behavior and appearance.

macOS Sonoma User's Guide

- **Configuring General Preferences**

The General Preferences tab is where you can control fundamental Finder settings. Here, you can adjust the behavior of new Finder windows, such as whether they should open to the previous location or a specific folder. You can also choose whether folders should open in a new window or replace the current one and whether to display external disks on the Desktop.

Additionally, this tab allows you to customize the appearance of icons, including their size and grid spacing, as well as turn on or off file extensions and Spring-loaded folders. This handy feature previews a folder's contents when you pause while dragging an item over it.

- **Tailoring the Sidebar**

In the Sidebar preferences tab, you can choose which items are displayed in the Sidebar, such as recent folders, shared folders, and iCloud Drive. You can also turn the Sidebar's integration on or off with third-party cloud storage services like Dropbox or Google Drive.

- **Customizing Advanced Settings**

The Advanced Preferences tab offers many options for power users and those seeking even more control over the Finder's behavior. Here, you can adjust settings related to file handling, such as displaying full path details in the title bar, enabling the warning before emptying the Trash, and setting up extensions to be removed when copying or duplicating files.

Also, this tab allows you to configure the behavior of the Finder window, such as enabling or disabling the warning before changing an extension or displaying the status bar at the bottom of the window.

- **Fine-Tuning Visual Cues**

The Finder's appearance can be customized through the Views tab to suit your visual preferences. Here, you can choose how files and folders are displayed, including options for icon size, grid spacing, and the visibility of various metadata fields like file size, date modified, and more.

You can also enable or deactivate visual cues like displaying icons for hidden files, displaying the user library folder, and showing the warning when changing a file extension.

Advanced Finder Tips and Tricks

Whether you're a seasoned Mac veteran or a newcomer to the platform, this guide will show you some advanced Finder tips and tricks that will transform how you interact with your files and folders.

- **The Power of Quick Look**

Quick Look is a feature that allows you to preview files without opening them fully. While many users are familiar with the Space bar shortcut to activate

Quick Look, there are lesser-known tricks that can further enhance your experience:

Quick Look Slideshows: Hold down the Option key while in Quick Look to reveal a toolbar with additional controls, including the ability to initiate a slideshow for image files or videos.

Quick Look Markup: For compatible file types, Quick Look allows you to annotate and markup files directly within the preview window, eliminating the need to open dedicated applications.

Quick Look Trimming: When previewing video files, you can use the trim controls to select and export specific video portions, which is perfect for quickly sharing clips or creating previews.

- **Advanced Search Techniques**

While the Finder's search functionality is powerful on its own, there are advanced techniques that can take your file-finding abilities to the next level:

Boolean Operators: Incorporate Boolean operators like "AND," "OR," and "NOT" to refine your search queries and locate specific files or folders with pinpoint accuracy.

Metadata Search: Use search attributes like "kind," "date," or "size" to filter your results based on specific file types, creation dates, or file sizes.

Saved Searches: Create and save complex search queries as Smart Folders, ensuring that your frequently used searches are just a click away.

- **Leveraging Terminal and Automation**

While the Finder offers a robust graphical user interface, power users can harness the command line and automation tools to supercharge their workflow:

Terminal Commands: Master essential Terminal commands like cp, mv, and rm to efficiently copy, move, and delete files and folders from the command line.

Automator Integration: Leverage Automator, macOS's built-in automation tool, to create custom workflows and automate repetitive tasks within the Finder.

AppleScript and Shell Scripts: Go into scripting with AppleScript or shell scripts to automate complex file management tasks and extend the Finder's functionality.

- **Enhancing the Finder Experience**

Beyond the built-in features, some third-party tools and utilities can further enhance your Finder experience:

Path Finder: This powerful third-party file manager offers advanced features like dual-pane browsing, batch renaming, and file management operations beyond the Finder's capabilities.

Default Folder X: This utility enhances the Open and Save dialogs, allowing you to navigate to frequently used folders and remember recent locations quickly.

TotalFinder: This innovative tool adds tabs, folders on top, and other productivity-boosting features to the Finder, transforming it into a more modern and efficient file manager.

The Finder is more than just a file browser – it's a gateway to optimized file management and a cornerstone of your Mac experience.

CHAPTER FIVE

Change Your Desktop Wallpaper

The first step in changing your desktop wallpaper is to access the Desktop & Screen Saver preference pane. Here's how:

Click on the **Apple menu** in the top-left corner of your screen. Select **"System Settings"** from the dropdown menu. In the System Settings window, click **"Desktop & Screen Saver"** in the sidebar.

Alternatively, you can use Spotlight search to access this pane quickly. Press Command + Space Bar to open Spotlight, then type "Desktop & Screen Saver" and press Return.

- **Wallpaper Options**

Once you're in the Desktop & Screen Saver preference pane, you'll be greeted with various wallpaper options. macOS Sonoma provides a curated collection of beautiful images across multiple categories, including:

Apple's stunning photography from around the world

Dynamic desktop pictures that subtly change throughout the day

Solid colors for a clean, minimalist look

A selection of abstract patterns and textures

Choosing Your Perfect Wallpaper

To set a new wallpaper, click on the thumbnail of your desired image in the preference pane. You'll see a live preview of how it will look on your desktop. If you'd like to use one of your photos, click the **"+" button** in the bottom-left corner, then navigate to the image you want.

macOS Sonoma introduces a new feature that allows you to set separate wallpapers for your desktop and lock screen. To access this option, click the **"Desktop"** or **"Lock Screen"** buttons at the top of the preference pane.

Customizing Your Wallpaper

Once you've selected your wallpaper, you can further customize its appearance. Click on the "**Options"** button to access settings for:

Scaling and positioning the image

Turning desktop picture rotation on or off

Setting a daily or hourly refresh interval for dynamic wallpapers

macOS Sonoma User's Guide

Change Your Screen Saver

Head to the Desktop & Screen Saver preference pane, where you'll find all the available options. Here's how:

Click on the **Apple menu** in the top-left corner of your screen. Select **"System Settings"** from the drop-down menu. In the System Settings window, click **"Desktop & Screen Saver"** in the sidebar.

Alternatively, you can use Spotlight search by pressing Command + Space Bar, typing "Desktop & Screen Saver," and pressing Return.

- **Choosing Your Screen Saver**

Once you're in the preference pane, you'll see a preview of the currently selected screen saver. To change it, click on the **"Screen Saver"** tab, then choose from the various options available:

Photo slideshows (including your photo library)

Apple's curated collections of nature scenes, cityscapes, and more

Classic screen savers like Flurry, Message, and Matrix

New additions in Sonoma, like the captivating Liquid and Cosmic animations

Many screen savers offer additional customization options. For example, with photo slideshows, you can adjust the transition speed and turn on or off features like shuffling and zooming.

Configuring Screen Saver Settings

In addition to choosing your screen saver, you can customize when and how it activates. Click on the "Screen Saver Options" button to access settings for:

Start screen saver after (set the idle time before the screen saver begins)

Show screen saver with display sleep (turn the screen saver on or off when your display sleeps)

Use Random Screen Saver (shuffle through different screen savers at each activation)

One of the standout features in macOS Sonoma is creating your screen saver from a video file. Drag and drop a compatible video file into the Screen Saver preference pane, and your Mac will automatically convert it into a mesmerizing, looping screen saver.

Add Widgets to Your Desktop

The first step in adding widgets to your desktop is to access the Desktop Widgets interface. Here's how:

Click on the **Apple menu** in the top-left corner of your screen. Select **"System Settings"** from the drop-down menu. Click "Desktop & Dock" in the sidebar in the System Settings window. In the Desktop & Dock preference pane, click on the "Desktop Widgets" tab.

Perry Hoover

Alternatively, you can use Spotlight search by pressing Command + Space Bar, typing "Desktop Widgets," and pressing Return.

- **The Widget Gallery**

Once you're in the Desktop Widgets interface, you'll be presented with a gallery of available widgets. These are divided into various categories, such as:

Weather and clock

Fitness and health tracking

News and information

productivity and utilities

And more

Each widget in the gallery provides a brief description and a preview of how it will appear on your desktop. You can also resize many widgets by clicking and dragging the corners of the preview.

macOS Sonoma User's Guide

- **Adding Widgets to Your Desktop**

To add a widget to your desktop, click the **"Add"** button next to the widget you want. The widget will immediately appear on your desktop, ready for you to position and customize.

You can add multiple widgets to your desktop, which will automatically be arranged in a grid layout. If you need to rearrange them, click and drag the widget to its desired location.

One of the standout features of Desktop Widgets in macOS Sonoma is the ability to create custom widgets from web content. Drag and drop a compatible web page or URL into the Desktop Widgets interface, and your Mac will automatically generate a widget displaying that content.

Organize Your Dock

The Dock is a prominent feature of the macOS desktop, providing quick access to your frequently used applications, files, and folders. It's designed to be a multi-purpose launchpad, allowing you to easily open, switch between, and manage your active apps. You can create a personalized workspace that suits your workflow by customising the Dock's appearance and behaviour.

- **Accessing the Dock Preferences**

To begin organizing your Dock, you must access the Dock preferences. There are several ways to do this:

System Preferences: Navigate to the Apple menu in the top-left corner of your screen, select "System Preferences," and then click on the "Dock" icon.

Dock Context Menu: Right-click (or Control-click) on the separator line that divides the Dock icons, and select "Dock Preferences" from the contextual menu.

Keyboard Shortcut: Press the Command + Option + D keys simultaneously to open the Dock preferences window directly.

- ## Customizing the Dock's Appearance

Once you've accessed the Dock preferences, you'll have various options to customize its appearance. Here are some of the key settings you can adjust:

Position on Screen: macOS Sonoma introduces a new feature that allows you to position the Dock on the left, right, or bottom edge of your screen, catering to your preferred workspace layout.

Size: Adjust the size of the Dock and its icons to your liking, ensuring a balance between visibility and screen real estate.

Magnification: Enable or turn off the magnification effect, which enlarges icons as you hover over them, making it easier to identify apps and documents.

- ## Managing Dock Icons

The true potential of the Dock is in its ability to organize and access your frequently used applications and files. Here's how you can manage the icons within your Dock:

Adding and Removing Icons: To add an application or file to the Dock, drag and drop it on it. To remove an icon, pull it off the Dock, and it will disappear in a puff of smoke.

Rearranging Icons: Rearrange your Dock icons by clicking and holding on an icon, then dragging it to your desired position within the Dock.

Folder Icons: You can create custom folders within the Dock to group related applications or files. Drag and drop one item onto another to create a folder.

Using Mission Control

Mission Control is a tool that provides a bird's-eye view of all your open applications, windows, and virtual desktops. It acts as a command center, enabling you to quickly switch between different workspaces, organize your cluttered screen, and move windows across desktops with a few simple gestures or keystrokes.

- **Accessing Mission Control**

There are several convenient ways to access Mission Control on your Mac:

Trackpad or Magic Mouse: With a swipe up using three or four fingers, Mission Control will appear, displaying all your open windows and desktops.

Keyboard Shortcut: Press the Control + Up Arrow keys simultaneously to invoke Mission Control.

Dock Icon: Click on the Mission Control icon in the Dock, typically represented by a rectangular grid or a set of overlapping rectangles.

Hot Corners: macOS Sonoma allows you to assign a specific corner of your screen as a Hot Corner for Mission Control. Move your cursor to the designated corner, and Mission Control will activate automatically.

- **Organizing Your Workspaces**

Once in Mission Control, you'll have a comprehensive view of all your open windows and desktops. Here's how you can take control of your workspaces:

Virtual Desktops: macOS Sonoma introduces a new feature that allows you to create and manage multiple virtual desktops, each with open applications and windows. It helps you categorize your work and reduce clutter.

Window Management: Easily drag and drop windows between desktops or use the keyboard shortcuts to move them around; this ensures that each desktop is dedicated to a specific task or project, enhancing your focus and productivity.

- **Navigating Between Desktops and Windows**

Switching Desktops: Click the desired desktop thumbnail in Mission Control or use the Control + Left/Right Arrow keyboard shortcuts to switch between virtual desktops.

Previewing Windows: Hover over a window thumbnail to get a larger preview of its contents, making it easier to identify and select the right window.

Closing Windows: In Mission Control, you can close any open window by hovering over its thumbnail and clicking the close button in the top-left corner.

- **Advanced Tips**

To further enhance your Mission Control experience, consider the following tips:

Keyboard Navigation: Use the arrow keys to navigate between desktops and windows while in Mission Control for a seamless, cursor-free experience.

Customization: Adjust the Mission Control preferences, such as changing the desktop layout, turning the preview feature on or off, and setting up Hot Corners to suit your workflow.

Integration with Spaces and Exposé: Mission Control seamlessly integrates with Spaces (for managing virtual desktops) and Exposé (for quickly accessing open windows within a single desktop), providing a comprehensive workspace management solution.

Using Launchpad

The Launchpad is a visually appealing and intuitive interface that displays all the applications installed on your Mac in a grid-like layout. This design makes it easy to quickly locate and launch the apps you need, eliminating the need to navigate through complex folder structures or cluttered desktops. With the Launchpad, your digital workspace becomes a well-organized and efficient environment.

- **Accessing the Launchpad**

There are several convenient ways to access the Launchpad on your Mac:

Dock Icon: Click on the Launchpad icon in the Dock, typically represented by a stylized rocket or grid of dots.

macOS Sonoma User's Guide

Keyboard Shortcut: Press the Pinch gesture on your trackpad with your thumb and three fingers, or use the keyboard shortcut Command + Space.

Spotlight Search: Type "Launchpad" in the search bar, and select the Launchpad option from the results.

Mission Control: While in Mission Control, click on the Launchpad thumbnail to enter the Launchpad interface directly.

- **Organizing Your Apps**

Once you've accessed the Launchpad, you'll have a grid of app icons. Here's how you can take control and organize your apps for maximum efficiency:

Automatic Organization: macOS Sonoma introduces a new feature that automatically organizes your apps into categories based on their type (e.g., Productivity, Social, Entertainment), making it easier to find and launch relevant apps.

Manual Arrangement: If you prefer a more personalized approach, you can manually rearrange the app icons by clicking and dragging them to your desired location within the Launchpad.

Spotlight Search: Search specific apps by typing their names in the Spotlight search bar at the Launchpad interface's top.

Managing Apps and Folders

Creating Folders: To create a new folder in the Launchpad, drag and drop one app icon onto another, and a folder will be automatically created, allowing you to group related apps.

Renaming Folders: Right-click (or Control-click) on a folder and select "Rename" to give it a descriptive name that reflects its contents.

Removing Apps: To remove an app from the Launchpad, click and drag the app icon towards the bottom of the screen until the "Remove" tooltip appears, then release the icon.

macOS Sonoma User's Guide

- **Advanced Tips**

To further enhance your Launchpad experience, consider the following tips:

Spotlight Search Integration: While in the Launchpad, you can use Spotlight Search to locate not only apps but also documents, contacts, and other files, making it a comprehensive productivity hub.

Gesture Navigation: Use multi-touch gestures on your trackpad or Magic Mouse to smoothly navigate the Launchpad pages, simulating a natural swiping motion.

Customization: Adjust the Launchpad preferences to suit your needs, such as changing the icon size, turning automatic app organization on or off, and setting up a custom app layout.

Using Dictation

Dictation is a speech-to-text tool that leverages advanced voice recognition algorithms to transcribe your spoken words into text accurately. This feature not only enhances accessibility for those who may have difficulty typing but also offers a convenient alternative for anyone seeking to boost their productivity and efficiency. With Dictation, you can seamlessly integrate voice input into your workflow, allowing you to capture your thoughts and ideas with remarkable ease.

- **Enabling Dictation**

You'll need to enable the feature to begin using Dictation on your Mac. There are several ways to do this:

System Preferences: Navigate to the Apple menu, select "System Preferences," and click the "Keyboard" icon. Under the "Dictation" tab, check the box next to "Enable Dictation."

macOS Sonoma User's Guide

Keyboard Shortcut: Press the Function (fn) key twice to toggle Dictation on or off quickly.

Dictation Toolbar: In supported applications, you'll find a "Dictation" toolbar icon that lets you turn the feature on or off with a single click.

Siri: Say, "Hey Siri, enable Dictation," and your virtual assistant will activate the feature for you.

- **Using Dictation**

Once Dictation is enabled, you can begin dictating your text. Here's how it works:

Voice Commands: macOS Sonoma introduces a new set of voice commands that allow you to control the Dictation feature seamlessly. For example, you can say "New Line" to start a new paragraph or "Period" to insert punctuation marks.

Continuous Dictation: With the latest update, Dictation can transcribe your speech in real-time, without pauses or additional prompts, providing a more natural and fluid experience.

Improved Accuracy: Apple has refined the voice recognition algorithms, enhancing accuracy and better handling of complex vocabulary, accents, and dialects.

Optimizing Your Dictation Experience

Microphone Setup: A high-quality microphone or headset is recommended for optimal performance. Ensure that your microphone is correctly configured in the **"Sound"** preferences.

Quiet Environment: Dictation works best in a calm environment with minimal background noise, ensuring accurate voice recognition and reducing errors.

Dictation Commands: Familiarize yourself with the available voice commands, such as "Cap" for capitalizing the next word or "Scratch That" to delete the last phrase.

- **Advanced Tips**

To further enhance your Dictation experience, consider the following tips:

Keyboard Shortcut Customization: Customize the keyboard shortcut for toggling Dictation on or off to suit your preferences.

Dictation Feedback: Enable "Dictation Feedback" in the Dictation preferences to see real-time transcription, making catching and correcting errors easier.

Accessibility Features: Explore the various accessibility options, such as speech-to-text and text-to-speech, to create a more inclusive and user-friendly experience.

CHAPTER SIX

Using Siri

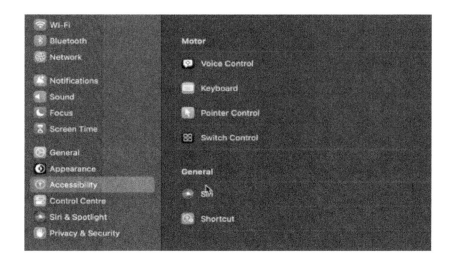

Siri has been a beloved companion on iOS devices for years. Now, it's ready to take your Mac experience to new heights. Imagine effortlessly controlling your Mac, launching apps, finding files, and getting things done with your voice. macOS Sonoma brings Siri to the forefront, integrating it deeply into the operating system for a seamless experience.

Accessing Siri on Your Mac

Before diving into the setup process, let's see how you can summon Siri on your Mac. With macOS Sonoma, Apple has made engaging with your virtual assistant easier than ever.

Keyboard Shortcut: Press and hold the Command + Space keys to activate Siri instantly. This method is perfect for those who prefer keyboard-based interactions.

Menu Bar Icon: Look for the Siri icon in your Mac's menu. A simple click will bring Siri to life, ready to assist you.

Voice Command: If you prefer a hands-free approach, say "Hey Siri" followed by your command. macOS Sonoma's enhanced microphone sensitivity ensures Siri can hear you clearly, even in noisy environments.

Setting Up Siri on macOS Sonoma

Now that you can access Siri let's dive into the setup process. Follow these simple steps to unlock Siri's full potential on your Mac:

Open the **Apple Menu** and select **System Settings**. Click on the Siri preference pane. Toggle the switch to enable Siri on your Mac.

Customize your **Voice Activation** settings by choosing the **"Hey Siri"** phrase or creating a custom voice command.

Adjust the Keyboard Shortcut if you prefer a different key combination.

Explore the Siri preference pane to familiarize yourself with options and settings.

- **Using Siri on Your Mac**

With Siri set up and ready to go, it's time to unleash its capabilities. Here are just a few examples of how Siri can revolutionize your Mac experience:

macOS Sonoma User's Guide

App Control: Launch apps, switch between running apps, or quit apps with simple voice commands like "Open Safari" or "Switch to Mail."

File Management: Locate files, documents, and folders by name or content. Siri can help you find what you need quickly and efficiently.

Web Searches: Ask Siri to search the web for information, images, or videos without leaving your current app.

Reminders and Notes: Create reminders, add items to your shopping list, or jot down quick notes using your voice.

System Controls: Adjust settings like brightness and volume or enable Do Not Disturb mode with a simple command.

Siri constantly learns and improves, so don't hesitate to observe its abilities and find new ways to enhance your productivity.

Using FaceTime for Video Calling

FaceTime, Apple's proprietary video calling app, offers macOS users a seamless and user-friendly experience.

- **Accessing FaceTime on Your Mac**

One of the beauties of FaceTime on macOS Sonoma is its seamless integration with the operating system. You can access the app in multiple ways, each designed to provide a smooth and convenient experience.

The first and most obvious method is through the **FaceTime app** icon, prominently displayed in the Dock. With a single click, you'll be whisked into the world of face-to-face conversations, ready to connect with friends, family, or colleagues.

Alternatively, you can summon FaceTime through the powerful Spotlight search feature. Press Command + Space Bar, type "FaceTime," and the app will appear, ready to launch with a single click or press the Return key.

macOS Sonoma User's Guide

Setting Up FaceTime for the First Time

If this is your first time using FaceTime on your Mac, you must complete a few simple setup steps. Don't worry; the process is straightforward and user-friendly.

You'll be prompted to sign in with your Apple ID upon launching FaceTime. This step is crucial, as it ensures that your FaceTime connections are secure and that you can seamlessly transition between your Apple devices, such as your iPhone or iPad.

Once signed in, FaceTime will ask for permission to access your Mac's camera and microphone. Grant these permissions, as they are essential for video and audio communication.

- **Adding Contacts to FaceTime**

You must add contacts to your list to initiate a FaceTime call. FaceTime intelligently integrates with your Mac's Contacts app, making connecting with people you already know easy.

Open the FaceTime app and click the **"+" button** in the top-left corner. You can search for contacts by name, email address, or phone number. As you type, FaceTime will suggest matching entries from your Contacts app.

Alternatively, you can add contacts directly from the Contacts app by selecting a contact and clicking the **"Add to FaceTime"** button.

- **Making a FaceTime Call**

With your contacts added, it's time to make your first FaceTime call on macOS Sonoma. The process is delightfully simple and intuitive.

In the FaceTime app, double-click on a contact's name or click the video camera icon next to their entry. FaceTime will initiate the call, and your camera and microphone will activate.

Suppose the person you're calling is available. Their video feed will appear on your screen, and you can start your face-to-face conversation. If they're unavailable or don't answer, you can leave a message or try again later.

- **Customizing FaceTime**

FaceTime on macOS Sonoma offers a range of customization options to enhance your video calling experience. For example, you can choose from various virtual backgrounds, adding a touch of personality or professionalism to your calls.

To access these options, click on the video camera icon in the FaceTime window during an active call. You can select a different camera (if multiple cameras are connected to your Mac), adjust video settings, or choose a virtual background.

Additionally, you can share your screen during a FaceTime call, making it an invaluable tool for remote collaboration, presentations, or tech support sessions. Click the **"Share Screen"** button in the FaceTime window, and your Mac's display will be shared with the other participants.

FaceTime's Unique Features on macOS

Sonoma

With each new iteration of macOS, Apple introduces unique features and enhancements to FaceTime, ensuring that the app remains at the forefront of video calling technology.

In macOS Sonoma, one of the standout features is the seamless integration with Apple's Continuity Camera. This innovative feature allows you to use your iPhone as a webcam for your Mac, providing superior video quality and flexibility.

To take advantage of this feature, ensure your iPhone and Mac are signed in with the same Apple ID and have Bluetooth and Wi-Fi enabled. During a FaceTime call, click on the video camera icon and select **"Use Continuity Camera."** Your iPhone's camera will automatically connect and provide a high-quality video feed.

Another unique feature of MacOS Sonoma is the ability to create FaceTime links. These shareable links allow you to initiate group calls quickly, making connecting with multiple participants simultaneously simpler than ever.

AirDrop

AirDrop is a proprietary file-sharing technology developed by Apple designed to facilitate data transfer between compatible devices wirelessly and securely.

Unlike traditional file transfer methods that require cables or network configurations, AirDrop relies on Bluetooth Low Energy (BLE) and Wi-Fi to establish a direct peer-to-peer connection between devices. This innovative approach eliminates the need for physical connections. It ensures that your data remains private and secure during the transfer process.

Enabling AirDrop on Your Mac

To begin using AirDrop on your Mac running macOS Sonoma, you must ensure the feature is enabled. Here's how you can do it:

Click on the **Apple menu** in the top-left corner of your screen and select **"System Settings."**

In the System Settings window, navigate to the **"General"** section and click **"AirDrop."**

In the AirDrop preferences, you'll see three options: "Receiving Off," "Contacts Only," and "Everyone." Choose the option that best suits your needs.

If you select "Contacts Only," you'll be able to receive files from people in your Contacts app. Alternatively, choosing "Everyone" will allow any nearby Apple device to detect and share files with your Mac.

macOS Sonoma User's Guide

Accessing AirDrop on macOS Sonoma

One of the most convenient ways to access AirDrop is through the Finder app. Open a Finder window, navigate to the "AirDrop" section in the sidebar, and see a list of nearby AirDrop-enabled devices.

Alternatively, you can access AirDrop directly from many apps, such as Photos, Notes, or Safari. Look for the **"Share"** button (often represented by a square with an upward-pointing arrow) and select "AirDrop" from the list of sharing options.

- **Sending Files with AirDrop**

With AirDrop at your fingertips, sharing files becomes a breeze. Let's walk through sending a file from your Mac to another AirDrop-enabled device.

Locate the file you want to share and open it in the appropriate app (e.g., Photos for images, Pages for documents).

Click the **"Share"** button and select **"AirDrop"** from the list of options.

Your Mac will scan for nearby devices with AirDrop enabled and display them in the AirDrop window.

Select the device you want to share the file with, and the recipient will receive a notification prompting them to accept or decline the transfer.

Once the recipient accepts, the file will transfer wirelessly and securely between your devices.

It's important to note that both devices must have AirDrop enabled and be within approximately 30 feet (9 meters) of each other for the transfer to be successful.

- **Receiving Files with AirDrop**

Just as sending files with AirDrop is seamless, receiving them is equally effortless. When someone attempts to share a file with your Mac via AirDrop, you'll see a notification appear on your screen.

macOS Sonoma User's Guide

This notification will display the name and profile picture (if available) of the person sending the file and a preview. From here, you can choose to accept or decline the transfer.

If you accept, the file will begin downloading to your Mac, and you'll receive another notification once the transfer is complete. By default, received files are stored in the "Downloads" folder on your Mac. You can still customize this location according to AirDrop preferences.

With each new iteration of macOS, Apple introduces unique enhancements and features to AirDrop, further improving the user experience. In macOS Sonoma, one of the standout features is the ability to share web URLs directly from Safari using AirDrop.

While browsing the web, click the "Share" button and select "AirDrop" to send the current URL to another device. This feature is handy for quickly sharing interesting articles, recipes, or online resources with friends and family.

Another unique aspect of AirDrop on macOS Sonoma is its integration with the new "Control Center" feature. Accessing the Control Center lets you quickly toggle AirDrop on or off and adjust your visibility settings without navigating multiple menus.

Handoff

Handoff is a technology that allows you to seamlessly transfer your work between Apple devices, such as your Mac, iPhone, or iPad. Whether you're working on a document, browsing the web, or consuming media, Handoff enables you to pick up exactly where you left off without missing a beat. This innovative feature relies on Bluetooth Low Energy (BLE) and Wi-Fi to establish a secure connection between your devices, ensuring your data remains private and protected throughout the transition process.

macOS Sonoma User's Guide

- **Enabling Handoff on Your Mac**

To begin using Handoff on your Mac running macOS Sonoma, you must ensure the feature is enabled on your Mac and other Apple devices. Here's how you can allow Handoff on your Mac:

Click on the Apple menu in the top-left corner of your screen and select **"System Settings."**

In the System Settings window, navigate to the **"General"** section and click **"Handoff."**

Toggle the "Handoff" switch to the **"On"** position.

Ensure your Mac and other Apple devices are signed in with the same Apple ID.

By enabling Handoff and using the same Apple ID across your devices, you can seamlessly transition between them, picking up where you left off.

Accessing Handoff on macOS Sonoma

With Handoff enabled, it's time to explore how to access and utilize this feature on your Mac. Apple has thoughtfully integrated Handoff into various areas of macOS Sonoma, making it easily accessible from multiple locations.

One of the most convenient ways to access Handoff is through the Dock. When you have an active app or activity on another Apple device, its icon appears in the Dock, accompanied by a small Handoff icon (a small rectangle with an upward-pointing arrow). Click on this icon, and the app or activity will seamlessly transition to your Mac, allowing you to continue right where you left off.

Alternatively, you can access Handoff through the Control Center on your Mac. Click on the Control Center icon in the menu bar (two rectangles with an upward-pointing arrow), and you'll see a list of available Handoff activities from your other devices.

- **Handing Off Your Work**

With Handoff at your fingertips, transitioning between your devices becomes a breeze. Let's walk through the process of handing off your work from one device to another.

Start working on an activity, such as writing a document, browsing the web, or editing a photo, on one of your Apple devices.

When you're ready to transition to another device, locate the Handoff icon (a small rectangle with an upward-pointing arrow) on the device you want to continue your work on.

Click or tap the Handoff icon, and the activity will seamlessly transfer to the new device, preserving your progress and allowing you to pick up right where you left off.

It's important to note that both devices must be connected to the same Wi-Fi network, have Bluetooth enabled, and be signed in with the same Apple ID for Handoff to work seamlessly.

With each new iteration of macOS, Apple introduces unique enhancements and features to Handoff, further improving the user experience. In macOS Sonoma, one of the standout features is the ability to hand off audio and video playback between your devices.

With Handoff, you can seamlessly transfer the playback to your iPhone or iPad, allowing you to continue watching without interruption. Suppose you're listening to a podcast on your iPhone and return to your Mac. In that case, you can easily hand off the audio playback to your computer, ensuring a seamless experience.

Another unique aspect of Handoff on macOS Sonoma is its integration with the new **"Universal Control"** feature. With Universal Control, you can use a single keyboard, mouse, or trackpad to control multiple Apple devices simultaneously, further enhancing your productivity and workflow.

Continuity Camera

Continuity Camera is a technology that allows you to use your iPhone as a wireless webcam for your

Mac, leveraging the advanced camera capabilities of your mobile device to provide superior video quality and versatility.

This innovative feature takes advantage of the seamless integration between Apple devices, relying on Bluetooth and Wi-Fi to establish a secure connection between your iPhone and Mac. With Continuity Camera, you can bid farewell to grainy, low-resolution webcams and embrace the power of your iPhone's advanced camera system.

- **Setting Up Continuity Camera**

To begin using Continuity Camera on your Mac running macOS Sonoma, you must ensure that both your Mac and iPhone meet the requirements and are appropriately configured. Here's how you can set up the Continuity Camera:

Ensure your Mac and iPhone are signed in with the same Apple ID.

On your Mac, navigate to **System Settings > General > Continuity Camera** and enable the "Continuity Camera" option.

On your iPhone, ensure that Bluetooth and Wi-Fi are enabled and your device is running the latest version of iOS.

Once these steps are complete, your Mac and iPhone will be ready to work together, providing you with a seamless and intuitive video-calling experience.

Accessing Continuity Camera on macOS Sonoma

With Continuity Camera set up, it's time to explore how to access and utilize this feature on your Mac. Apple has thoughtfully integrated Continuity Camera into various apps and scenarios, making it easily accessible and convenient.

One of the most common ways to access Continuity Camera is through video conferencing apps like FaceTime or Zoom. When you join a video call, click on the video settings or camera selection menu to see your iPhone listed as an available camera option. Select your iPhone, and the app will seamlessly switch to your mobile device's camera, providing superior video quality.

Alternatively, you can access Continuity Camera through the Control Center on your Mac. Click on the **Control Center icon** in the menu bar to find the **"Continuity Camera"** option, allowing you to quickly turn the feature on or off with a single click.

- **The Power of Continuity Camera**

With Continuity Camera at your fingertips, you can release the complete potential of your video calls, presentations, and virtual interactions. Here are just a few ways you can leverage this innovative feature:

Enhanced Video Quality: Bid farewell to grainy, low-resolution webcams and embrace the stunning clarity and detail of your iPhone's advanced camera system. Whether participating in a video conference or recording a tutorial, Continuity Camera will ensure you look your best.

Multi-purpose Camera Angles: Break free from the constraints of a fixed webcam position by using your iPhone as a mobile camera. Move your iPhone to capture different angles and perspectives, adding a dynamic and engaging element to your presentations or video calls.

Portrait Mode and Depth Effects: Take advantage of your iPhone's advanced camera features, such as Portrait Mode and Depth Effects, to create a beautiful, professional-looking background blur effect. It will help you stand out and command attention during your virtual interactions.

Desktop View: With Continuity Camera, you can seamlessly switch between your iPhone's camera and your Mac's built-in camera, allowing you to easily share your desktop screen or switch between camera views during a presentation or video call.

macOS Sonoma User's Guide

With each new iteration of macOS, Apple introduces unique enhancements and features to Continuity Camera, further improving the user experience. In macOS Sonoma, one of the standout features is the ability to use your iPhone's Ultra Wide camera for an even wider field of view.

Imagine being able to capture an entire conference room or classroom during a video call, providing a more immersive and inclusive experience for your colleagues or students. The Ultra Wide camera option lets you easily switch between different camera perspectives, ensuring that everyone is included and no detail is missed.

Another unique aspect of Continuity Camera on macOS Sonoma is its integration with the new "Desk View" feature. With Desk View, you can use your iPhone's camera to capture a top-down view of your desk or workspace, making sharing documents, sketches, or physical objects easier during a video call or presentation.

Universal Clipboard

Universal Clipboard is a technology that allows you to seamlessly copy and paste text, images, and other content across your Apple devices, ensuring that your workflows effortlessly between your Mac, iPhone, and iPad. This feature relies on Bluetooth Low Energy (BLE) and Wi-Fi to establish a secure connection between your devices, ensuring your data remains private and protected throughout the transfer process. With Universal Clipboard, you can say goodbye to the hassle of emailing files to yourself or manually retyping content across devices.

- **Enabling Universal Clipboard on Your Mac**

To begin using Universal Clipboard on your Mac running macOS Sonoma, you'll need to ensure the feature is enabled on both your Mac and your other Apple devices. Here's how you can allow Universal Clipboard on your Mac:

macOS Sonoma User's Guide

Click on the **Apple menu** in the top-left corner of your screen and select **"System Settings."**

In the System Settings window, navigate to the **"General"** section and click **"Universal Clipboard."**

Toggle the "Universal Clipboard" switch to the **"On"** position.

Ensure your Mac and other Apple devices are signed in with the same Apple ID.

By enabling Universal Clipboard and using the same Apple ID across your devices, you can seamlessly transfer content between them, streamlining your workflow and boosting productivity.

Accessing Universal Clipboard on macOS Sonoma

With Universal Clipboard enabled, it's time to explore how to access and utilize this feature on your Mac. Apple has thoughtfully integrated Universal Clipboard into various apps and scenarios, making it easily accessible and intuitive.

One of the most common ways to access Universal Clipboard is through the standard copy-and-paste keyboard shortcuts. Copy content on one device (e.g., your iPhone or iPad) using the familiar "Copy" command, and then paste it on your Mac using the "Paste" shortcut (Command + V). The content seamlessly transfers between your devices, eliminating the need for additional steps or file transfers.

Alternatively, you can access Universal Clipboard through the "Edit" menu in most apps on your Mac. Look for the "Paste" option, and you'll see a list of recently copied items from your other devices, allowing you to select and paste the desired content with a single click.

- **Leveraging Universal Clipboard's Capabilities**

macOS Sonoma User's Guide

With Universal Clipboard at your fingertips, you can streamline your workflow and boost your productivity in countless ways. Here are just a few scenarios where this innovative feature can prove invaluable:

Seamless Text Transfer: Copy a passage of text from a website or document on your iPhone and paste it directly into a report or presentation on your Mac: no more tedious retyping or emailing text to yourself.

Image and Media Sharing: Capture a stunning photo or record a video on your iPhone, copy it to the clipboard, and effortlessly paste it into a document, email, or presentation on your Mac. Say goodbye to the hassle of manually transferring media files between devices.

Cross-Device Collaboration: Working on a group project or collaborating with colleagues? Universal Clipboard allows you to seamlessly share content between your devices, ensuring everyone can access the latest information, regardless of their device.

Efficient Multitasking: Seamlessly transition between tasks and devices without losing your place. Copy a URL or snippet of code on your Mac, switch to your iPad or iPhone, and paste it directly into the appropriate app, saving valuable time and effort.

- **Universal Clipboard's Unique Features on macOS Sonoma**

With each new iteration of macOS, Apple introduces unique enhancements and features to Universal Clipboard, further improving the user experience. In macOS Sonoma, one of the standout features is the ability to copy and paste rich content, such as formatted text, images, and even video clips, while preserving their original formatting and quality.

Another unique aspect of Universal Clipboard on macOS Sonoma is its integration with the new "Universal Control" feature. With Universal Control,

macOS Sonoma User's Guide

you can use a single keyboard, mouse, or trackpad to control multiple Apple devices simultaneously, further enhancing your productivity and workflow. Combine this with Universal Clipboard, and you can effortlessly move content between devices with just a few clicks or taps.

CHAPTER SEVEN

What is an Apple ID?

Your Apple ID is your personalized gateway to many of Apple's services and applications. You can effortlessly access the App Store, iCloud, iMessage, FaceTime, and many more with a single set of credentials. This centralized approach streamlines your digital life, eliminating the need to remember multiple usernames and passwords for each service.

macOS Sonoma User's Guide

- **Syncing and Seamless Integration**

One of the most compelling features of the Apple ID is its ability to sync your data across multiple Apple devices seamlessly. Whether working on a document, browsing the web, or managing your calendar, your information is automatically kept up-to-date and accessible on all your connected devices. This level of integration ensures a consistent and cohesive experience, allowing you to pick up right where you left off, no matter which device you're using.

- **Personalization and Customization**

You can customize your Mac with an Apple ID to suit your unique preferences and needs. From configuring system settings to organizing your desktop and dock layout, your Apple ID serves as a digital fingerprint, ensuring your Mac feels like an extension of your style and workflow.

To access the Apple ID on your Mac, sign in with your credentials during the initial setup process or visit the **"System Preferences"** app and navigate to the **"Apple ID"** section. You can manage your account settings, security preferences, and connected devices here.

Apple continuously updates and enhances the features and capabilities associated with the Apple ID, ensuring you can always access the latest and most incredible offerings.

Set Up Your Apple ID

Step 1: Access the Apple ID Setup

During the initial setup of your Mac, you'll be prompted to sign in with your Apple ID or create a new one. If you've already skipped this step or need to modify your Apple ID settings, navigate to the **"System Preferences"** application and click the **"Apple ID"** icon.

macOS Sonoma User's Guide

Step 2: Sign In or Create a New Apple ID

If you already have an Apple ID, enter your credentials and follow the on-screen instructions to sign in. If you're new to the Apple ecosystem, click the **"Create Apple ID"** button and follow the prompts to set up a new account. This process will guide you through entering your personal information, setting a secure password, and configuring your security questions.

Step 3: Configure Your Account Settings

Once you're signed in, you can access various account settings and preferences. Here, you can customize your iCloud storage plan, manage your payment and shipping information, and control which services and applications are synced across your devices.

Step 4: Enable Two-Factor Authentication

Now, to enhance the security of your Apple ID, it is highly recommended that two-factor authentication be enabled. This additional layer of protection ensures that even if someone obtains your password, they won't be able to access your account without a trusted device or verification code.

You can access and manage your Apple ID settings anytime by navigating to the "System Preferences" application and clicking the "Apple ID" icon. This centralized location lets you update your personal information, review your connected devices, and adjust your privacy and security settings.

iCloud Overview

iCloud is a cloud-based service that seamlessly integrates with macOS, providing a comprehensive suite of features designed to enhance productivity, facilitate collaboration, and ensure your data is always accessible and up-to-date across all your Apple devices. This ecosystem offers a seamless and integrated experience, making it an essential part of the macOS environment.

- **iCloud Drive: Your Cloud Storage**

At the heart of the iCloud ecosystem is iCloud Drive, a cloud-based storage solution allowing you to access and manage your files from anywhere, anywhere, on any device. With iCloud Drive, you can easily store and sync documents, photos, videos, and other files, ensuring that your most important data is always accessible and up-to-date, regardless of your device.

- **iCloud Photo Library: Preserving Your Memories**

Keeping your cherished memories safe and organized has never been easier with iCloud Photo Library. This feature automatically uploads and syncs your photos and videos across all your Apple devices, ensuring your entire photo library is always at your fingertips. With intelligent search capabilities and seamless integration with the Photos app on macOS, managing and reliving your memories becomes a delightful experience.

- **iCloud Keychain: Secure and Convenient Password Management**

Managing multiple passwords can be unnerving in today's digital age. iCloud Keychain simplifies this process by securely storing your website login credentials, Wi-Fi passwords, and other sensitive information and syncing them across all your Apple devices. With iCloud Keychain, you can easily access your accounts without the hassle of remembering countless passwords.

Accessing the iCloud ecosystem on your Mac is seamless and intuitive. Sign in with your Apple ID during the initial setup process, and your Mac will automatically sync with iCloud, ensuring that your data is always up-to-date and accessible across all your devices. You can also manage your iCloud settings and preferences by navigating to the "System Preferences" application and clicking the "Apple ID" icon.

Apple continuously enhances the iCloud ecosystem, introducing new features and services to improve productivity and collaboration. One of the latest additions is iCloud+, which includes advanced privacy features such as Private Relay and Hide My Email, further safeguarding your online activities and personal information.

Use iCloud Drive

With iCloud Drive, your data is always up-to-date, secure, and accessible, making it an essential tool for modern computing.

Step 1: Enable iCloud Drive

Before using iCloud Drive, you must ensure it's enabled on your Mac. To do this, navigate to the "System Preferences" application and click the "Apple ID" icon. Check the "iCloud" option in the "iCloud Drive" section.

Step 2: Access iCloud Drive

Once iCloud Drive is enabled, you can access it in several ways:

Through the Finder: You'll see an iCloud Drive icon in the Finder sidebar. Click on it to access your iCloud Drive files and folders.

From the iCloud Drive folder: In the Finder, navigate to the "iCloud Drive" folder, which is typically located in your home directory.

From within compatible apps: Many apps, such as Pages, Numbers, and Keynote, offer direct integration with iCloud Drive, allowing you to open and save files directly to and from the cloud.

Step 3: Manage Your Files

With iCloud Drive, you can easily create, upload, and manage your files and folders as you would with a local storage drive. Drag and drop files into iCloud Drive, create new folders, or open and edit existing documents. Any changes you make will be automatically synced across all your devices, ensuring you always have access to the latest versions of your files.

Step 4: Share and Collaborate

One of the powerful features of iCloud Drive is the ability to share files and collaborate with others. Right-click on a file or folder and select "Share" to generate a shareable link or invite specific people to collaborate. This feature is convenient for group projects, allowing multiple users to work on the same document simultaneously.

Accessing iCloud Drive on your Mac is seamless and intuitive. Once enabled, you can find it in the Finder sidebar, the iCloud Drive folder in your home directory, or within compatible apps. Additionally, you can manage your iCloud Drive settings and preferences by navigating to the "System Preferences" application and clicking on the "Apple ID" icon.

One of the latest additions is the ability to create shared folders, which allows you to easily share and collaborate on entire folders with others, streamlining the process of managing group projects or shared resources.

Set Up Family Sharing

Family Sharing is a feature in macOS that allows you to seamlessly share purchases, subscriptions, and other content across multiple Apple devices within your family group. By setting up Family Sharing, you can create a unified digital environment where everyone can access and enjoy the same apps, music, movies, and more while maintaining individual accounts and privacy.

Step 1: Set Up Family Sharing

To get started with Family Sharing, open the "System Preferences" application and click on the "Family Sharing" icon. If you haven't set up Family Sharing, click the "Set Up Family" button and follow the on-screen instructions.

macOS Sonoma User's Guide

Step 2: Create a Family Group

You'll be prompted to create a new family group or join an existing one during setup. If you're setting up Family Sharing for the first time, choose the "Create a New Family" option and follow the steps to invite family members to join your group.

Step 3: Invite Family Members

You'll need their Apple ID and email addresses to invite family members to your Family Sharing group. Once you've entered their information, they'll receive an invitation to join your family group. Family members can choose to accept or decline the invitation.

Step 4: Share Purchases and Subscriptions

One of the key benefits of Family Sharing is the ability to share purchased content across devices. Once your family group is set up, you can share app purchases, iCloud storage, Apple Music subscriptions, and more. It ensures that everyone in your family can access the same content without purchasing it multiple times.

Step 5: Set Up Parental Controls

For families with children, Family Sharing also offers robust parental control features. As the family organizer, you can manage and monitor your children's device usage, app installations, and content access. It ensures a safe and age-appropriate digital environment for your kids.

After setting it up, you can manage your family group settings by navigating to the "System Preferences" application and clicking the "Family Sharing" icon. Add or remove family members, adjust shared content settings, and configure parental controls here.

One of the latest additions is the ability to share Apple Arcade and Apple TV+ subscriptions with your family group, allowing everyone to enjoy the latest games and shows on their devices.

macOS Sonoma User's Guide

Share Purchases with Your Family

Step 1: Ensure Family Sharing is Set Up

Before sharing purchases, you must ensure that Family Sharing is appropriately set up on your Mac. If you haven't already done so, follow these steps:

Open the "System Preferences" application and click the "Family Sharing" icon.

Click on the "Set Up Family" button and follow the on-screen instructions to create a new family group or join an existing one.

Invite family members to join your group by providing their Apple IDs and email addresses.

Step 2: Choose What to Share

Once your family group is set up, you can choose which types of purchases you want to share. Here's how:

In the "System Preferences" app, click on the "Family Sharing" icon.

Under the "Purchase Sharing" section, check the boxes following the types of content you want to share, such as "App Store Purchases," "iCloud Storage," or "Apple Music Subscriptions."

Step 3: Start Sharing Purchases

With the configuring sharing settings, you and your family can now access and download shared purchases on your respective devices. Here's how it works:

Open the App Store, iTunes Store, or Apple Books on your Mac.

Browse or search for the content you want to download.

Suppose another family member has already purchased the content. In that case, you'll see a "Download" or "Install" button instead of a "Buy" button.

Click the "Download" or "Install" button to access the shared content.

macOS Sonoma User's Guide

Use Messages with Your Family

Family Sharing lets you stay connected with your loved ones through Apple services, including iMessage.

Step 1: Set Up Family Sharing

Before using iMessage with your family, you must ensure that Family Sharing is appropriately set up on your Mac. If you haven't done so already, follow these steps:

Open the "System Preferences" application and click the "Family Sharing" icon.

Click on the "Set Up Family" button and follow the on-screen instructions to create a new family group or join an existing one.

Invite family members to join your group by providing their Apple IDs and email addresses.

Step 2: Enable iMessage for Family Sharing

Once your family group is set up, you can enable iMessage for Family Sharing. Here's how:

In the "System Preferences" app, click on the "Family Sharing" icon.

Under the "Share" section, check the box next to "iMessage."

Follow any additional prompts to confirm your settings.

Step 3: Start Using iMessage with Your Family

With iMessage enabled for Family Sharing, you and your family can now communicate seamlessly using iMessage on your respective devices. Here's how it works:

Open the "Messages" app on your Mac.

Create a new conversation or open an existing one with your family members.

Type your message and press "Enter" to send it.

macOS Sonoma User's Guide

Your family members will receive your message on their devices, and you can continue the conversation just as you would with any other iMessage conversation.

Accessing and managing Family Sharing on your Mac is straightforward. Navigate to the "System Preferences" application and click the "Family Sharing" icon. You can turn shared services on or off, like iMessage, from here and add or remove family members from your group.

One of the latest additions is the ability to use Family Sharing for screen time management. It allows parents to limit and restrict their children's app usage and device time, even when they're not physically together.

Share iCloud Storage with Your Family

With Family Sharing on macOS, you can take advantage of a unique feature that allows you to share your iCloud Storage plan with your family members, eliminating the need for each person to purchase their storage plan.

Step 1: Ensure Family Sharing is Set Up

Before sharing your iCloud Storage, you must ensure that Family Sharing is correctly configured on your Mac. If you haven't already done so, follow these steps:

Open the "System Preferences" application and click the "Family Sharing" icon.

Click on the "Set Up Family" button and follow the on-screen instructions to create a new family group or join an existing one.

Invite family members to join your group by providing their Apple IDs and email addresses.

Step 2: Enable iCloud Storage Sharing

You can enable iCloud Storage sharing once your family group is set up. Here's how:

macOS Sonoma User's Guide

In the "System Preferences" app, click on the "Family Sharing" icon.

Under the "Share" section, check the box next to "iCloud Storage."

Follow any additional prompts to confirm your settings.

Step 3: Manage Your Family's iCloud Storage

With iCloud Storage sharing enabled, you and your family can now access and utilize the shared storage plan. Here's how to manage and monitor your family's iCloud Storage usage:

Open the "Apple ID" section in "System Preferences."

Click on the "Manage Family Storage" option.

From here, you can view the storage usage of each family member and adjust their storage allowances as needed.

One of the latest additions is the ability to share and collaborate on iCloud Drive folders with your family members, allowing you to work together on projects and easily share files and documents.

CHAPTER EIGHT

Open and Close Safari

The most conventional way to summon Safari is through the iconic Dock, a staple of the macOS interface. You can effortlessly launch the browser with a simple click on the vibrant compass icon. This method is not only straightforward but also deeply ingrained in the muscle memory of countless Mac users.

- **The Spotlight Approach: Swift and Efficient**

If you're seeking an even quicker route, macOS offers the versatile Spotlight search feature. By pressing the Command + Space bar combination, you can invoke the Spotlight window and type "Safari." In an instant, the browser's icon will appear, ready for you to launch it with a single click or by pressing the Return key. This approach is convenient when your Dock is overcrowded, or you need to access Safari swiftly amidst a flurry of open applications.

- **Siri, the Virtual Assistant**

In the era of voice-controlled assistants, macOS users can harness the power of Siri to open Safari effortlessly. Invoke Siri by pressing the designated vital combination (often Command + Space bar), clicking on the Siri icon in the menu bar, and uttering the command "Hey Siri, open Safari." Siri will promptly comply, launching the browser for your convenience.

macOS Sonoma User's Guide

No matter which method you choose, closing Safari is equally straightforward. You can click on the red "close" button in the top-left corner of the window or use the keyboard shortcut Command + Q. Additionally, you can right-click (or Control + click) on the Safari icon in the Dock and select "Quit" from the contextual menu.

One unique aspect of Safari on macOS Sonoma is its seamless integration with other Apple devices through the Continuity feature. If you have an iPhone or iPad signed in with the same Apple ID, you can effortlessly pick up where you left off on your Mac or vice versa. Safari will automatically sync your browsing history, open tabs, and reading lists across all your devices, ensuring a cohesive experience.

Navigate the Web Using the Toolbar and Bookmarks

The toolbar in Safari is a veritable Swiss Army knife packed with essential tools to streamline your browsing experience. With a simple glance, you can access the address bar, quickly switch between tabs, and even customize the toolbar to suit your preferences.

To begin, let's familiarize ourselves with the toolbar's layout. On the left, you'll find the back and forward buttons, allowing you to retrace your steps or forge ahead easily. Beside them lies the address bar, where you can enter URLs or initiate searches with a few keystrokes.

- **Customizing the Toolbar for Efficiency**

One of the standout features of Safari on macOS Sonoma is the ability to tailor the toolbar to your specific needs. Right-click (or Control+click) on the toolbar and select **"Customize Toolbar"** to unveil many options. You can add or remove icons for

macOS Sonoma User's Guide

features like Reader View, Sidebar, and extensions, ensuring your most-used tools are always within reach.

- **The Power of Bookmarks**

In the age of information overload, bookmarks have become indispensable for keeping track of your favorite websites and online resources. Safari on macOS Sonoma offers a robust bookmarking system that seamlessly integrates with your browsing experience.

To bookmark a website, click the Share icon in the toolbar and select **"Add Bookmark."** Alternatively, you can use the keyboard shortcut Command+D to add the current page to your bookmarks quickly. Safari will automatically suggest a folder based on the website's content. Still, you can also create custom folders to organize your bookmarks as you see fit.

Accessing your bookmarks is equally effortless. Click on the Sidebar icon in the toolbar to unveil a comprehensive list of your bookmarks, neatly organized by folders. You can even search for specific bookmarks using the search bar at the top of the Sidebar.

If you seek a more visual approach, Safari's Favorites Bar offers a convenient way to access your most frequently visited websites with a single click. Drag and drop bookmarks from the Sidebar onto the Favorites Bar, and they'll be readily available along the toolbar.

One of the standout features in macOS Sonoma is the introduction of Shared Bookmarks. With this innovative functionality, you can effortlessly share bookmarks with other Apple devices logged in with the same iCloud account. Whether transitioning from your iPhone to your Mac or collaborating with colleagues, your bookmarks will seamlessly sync across devices, ensuring a consistent browsing experience no matter where you are.

Search For Information on The Web

Effective web searching begins with the address bar, a simple tool that packs a punch. In Safari on macOS Sonoma, the address bar doubles as a search field, allowing you to type in your queries and instantly receive relevant results from various search engines.

Type your keywords into the address bar and press Enter for a basic search. Safari will automatically detect your preferred search engine and present you with a curated list of relevant websites, articles, and media related to your query.

- **Refining Your Search: Advanced Techniques**

While basic searches can yield satisfactory results, Safari on macOS Sonoma offers a suite of advanced search operators that can elevate your search game to new heights. These operators act as filters, helping you narrow your search and retrieve more precise information.

For instance, enclosing a phrase in quotation marks (e.g., "macOS Sonoma search tips") instructs Safari to look for that exact phrase, ensuring your results are concrete. Additionally, you can use the minus sign (-) to exclude specific terms from your search, effectively filtering out unwanted content.

- **Tapping into Smart Search Fields**

One of the standout features of Safari on macOS Sonoma is its ability to recognize and interpret specific types of searches. When you enter queries related to calculations, unit conversions, or dictionary definitions, Safari intelligently acknowledges these. It presents you with the relevant information directly in the search results.

For example, typing "5 miles to kilometers" into the address bar will instantly display the conversion result, saving you the hassle of navigating a separate website or application.

Accessing these search capabilities is as simple as opening Safari and interacting with the address

macOS Sonoma User's Guide

bar. Whether using a keyboard shortcut (Command + L) or clicking directly in the address bar, Safari is ready to process your queries quickly and accurately.

Furthermore, you can customize your search preferences by navigating to Safari's settings, selecting your preferred search engine, or enabling additional search providers for specific queries.

One of the unique aspects of searching in Safari on macOS Sonoma is its deep integration with Siri. You can initiate web searches using natural language by invoking Siri with a simple voice command or keyboard shortcut. Siri will understand your query and present the results directly in Safari, providing a seamless and hands-free browsing experience.

Additionally, with the introduction of Live Text in macOS Sonoma, you can now search for and interact with text within images displayed in Safari. Hover over an image, and Safari will intelligently recognize and highlight any text it contains, allowing you to search for more information or take further actions based on that text.

Use Tabs to Manage Multiple Websites

The tab bar in Safari is the command center for your browsing experience. Located at the top of the window, it displays all your currently open websites, each represented by a sleek and visually distinct tab. You can quickly identify and switch between different pages with a single glance, keeping your workflow organized and clutter-free.

To open a new tab, click on the **"+" icon** at the far right of the tab bar or use the keyboard shortcut Command + T. This will instantly create a fresh canvas ready to explore new online destinations.

- **Customizing Tab Behavior**

Safari on macOS Sonoma offers many customization options to tailor your tab experience to your preferences. Right-click (or Control+click) on the tab bar to access a range of settings; this includes showing website favicons in tabs, enabling tab previews, and even controlling how new tabs are opened and positioned.

For those who prefer a more minimalistic approach, Safari allows you to hide the tab bar entirely, freeing up valuable screen real estate. Right-click on the tab bar and select **"Hide Tab Bar"** to declutter your browsing environment.

- **Organizing Your Tabs**

As your browsing session progresses, you may juggle multiple tabs simultaneously. Safari on macOS Sonoma provides several tools to help you maintain order amidst the chaos. One such tool is the ability to group related tabs, ensuring your workflow remains organized and focused.

To create a tab group, right-click on any tab and select **"New Tab Group with Selected Tabs."** You can then assign a name and color to this group, making it easy to identify and switch between different contexts or projects.

Accessing and navigating tabs in Safari is a breeze, with multiple methods at your disposal. The keyboard shortcut **Command + Shift + [** or **]** lets you quickly cycle through open tabs. At the same time, Command + Option + Right Arrow or Left Arrow moves your focus between individual tabs.

For those who prefer a more visual approach, the tab overview feature offers a bird's-eye view of all your open tabs. Press the **Command + Shift + ** shortcut, or click the **"Show Tab Overview"** button in the toolbar to unveil a comprehensive grid of all your tabs, making it easy to identify and switch to the desired website.

One of the standout features of Safari on macOS Sonoma is its seamless integration with other Apple devices through the Continuity feature. With Handoff, you can seamlessly transition your browsing experience between your Mac, iPhone, or iPad, picking up right where you left off with all your open tabs intact. It means you can start researching on your Mac and continue browsing the same tabs on your iPad while on the go, ensuring a cohesive and uninterrupted web experience.

Save Your Favorite Websites as Bookmarks

Effective bookmarking begins with a simple yet powerful action: adding a website to your collection. In Safari on macOS Sonoma, this process is as straightforward as it is intuitive. While browsing a webpage you wish to bookmark, locate the Share icon in the toolbar (or press Command + D) and select **"Add Bookmark."**

Safari will automatically suggest a name and location for your new bookmark. Still, you can easily customize these details to your liking. The choice is yours whether you prefer a concise or more descriptive title.

- **Organizing Your Bookmarks**

As your collection of bookmarks grows, maintaining an organized structure becomes paramount. Safari on macOS Sonoma offers a comprehensive bookmarks manager, accessible by clicking on the toolbar's Sidebar icon or pressing Command + Option + B.

Within the bookmarks manager, you'll find a hierarchical structure of folders and subfolders, allowing you to group related websites. To create a new folder, click the **"+" icon** at the bottom of the sidebar and select **"New Folder."** You can then drag and drop existing bookmarks into these folders or even nest folders within folders for a more granular organization.

- **Streamlining Access with the Favorites Bar**

Safari on macOS Sonoma offers a convenient shortcut for websites you frequent regularly: the Favorites Bar. This customizable toolbar, located just below the main toolbar, provides easy access to your most visited sites with a single click.

To add a bookmark to the Favorites Bar, locate it in the bookmarks manager and drag it onto the Favorites Bar. You can rearrange the order of these bookmarks by dragging and dropping them into your preferred positions, ensuring that your most essential online destinations are always within reach.

Accessing your bookmarks in Safari is a seamless experience, with multiple avenues at your disposal. Beyond the bookmarks manager and Favorites Bar, you can quickly access your bookmarks by clicking on the Share icon in the toolbar and selecting "Bookmarks." It will present you with a comprehensive list of bookmarked websites organized by folder structure.

Additionally, Safari on macOS Sonoma offers a dedicated bookmarks menu, accessible by clicking the **"Bookmarks"** option in the main menu bar. This menu is a convenient shortcut to your most frequently visited sites and a gateway to the full bookmarks manager.

With the introduction of Shared Bookmarks in macOS Sonoma, you can now collaborate and share bookmarks with others, fostering a collaborative browsing experience perfect for teams or families.

CHAPTER NINE

Create and Organize Notes

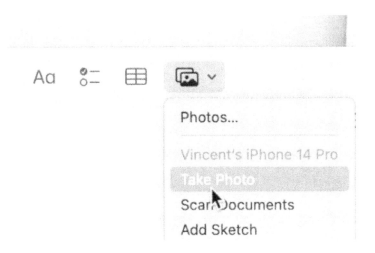

The Notes app in macOS Sonoma is conveniently located in the Applications folder, making it easily accessible with just a few clicks. Alternatively, you can use the Spotlight search feature by pressing Command + Space and typing "Notes" to launch the app instantly.

- **Creating a New Note**

To create a new note, click on the **"New Note"** button in the top left corner of the Notes app or use the keyboard shortcut Command + N. It will open a blank canvas where you can start typing or adding various types of content, such as text, images, sketches, or scanned documents.

One of the standout features of the Notes app is its intuitive formatting toolbar, which allows you to easily format your text with different styles, fonts, and colors. You can insert checklists and tables or create beautiful handwritten notes using your trackpad.

- **Organizing Your Notes**

As your collection of notes grows, organization becomes crucial. macOS Sonoma offers several ways to keep your notes tidy and easily accessible.

For instance, you can create folders to group related notes together. Right-click in the sidebar and select **"New Folder"** to create a new folder, then drag and drop your notes into the appropriate folders.

Additionally, you can use tags to categorize your notes based on specific topics, projects, or priorities.

macOS Sonoma User's Guide

To add a tag, type the # symbol followed by the tag name within the note's body or in the tag field at the top of the note.

Embracing the Power of Multimedia

The Notes app in macOS Sonoma isn't just limited to text. You can effortlessly incorporate multimedia elements into your notes, such as images, videos, or audio recordings. This feature is handy for capturing visual references, recording lectures, or documenting creative ideas.

For instance, if you're taking notes during a meeting or lecture, you can easily add a video or audio recording by clicking the respective buttons in the toolbar; this ensures you don't miss any important details and can revisit the multimedia content whenever necessary.

Type, Draw, or Insert Images into Your Notes

Launch the Notes app by clicking its Dock icon or searching for it using Spotlight (Command + Space). Once the app opens, you can create a new note by clicking the "New Note" button or using the keyboard shortcut Command + N.

- **Typing Your Notes**

The most conventional way to take notes is by typing. The Notes app in macOS Sonoma provides a distraction-free writing environment with a sleek and user-friendly interface. Click within the note's body and start typing.

To enhance your typing experience, it offers a comprehensive formatting toolbar that allows you to apply different text styles, fonts, and colors. You can also create bulleted or numbered lists and indents and apply various formatting options to make your notes more organized and visually appealing.

macOS Sonoma User's Guide

- ## **Drawing or Handwriting Your Notes**

MacOS Sonoma's Notes app supports drawing and handwriting for those who prefer a more hands-on approach. This feature is suitable for sketching diagrams, taking visual notes, or capturing ideas more creatively and intuitively.

Imagine you're an architect or designer attending a meeting. With the drawing tools in the Notes app, you can quickly sketch out your ideas or annotate existing images, allowing you to communicate your concepts more effectively.

To access the drawing tools, click the pencil icon in the toolbar or use the keyboard shortcut Command + Option + P. You can choose from various pen and highlighter tools, adjust the line thickness and color, and switch between writing and drawing modes.

- ## **Inserting Images into Your Notes**

In addition to typing and drawing, the Notes app allows you to insert images into your notes, providing a more comprehensive and visually appealing note-taking experience.

To insert an image, click on the camera icon in the toolbar or use the keyboard shortcut Command + Control + I. From there, you can take a new photo or video using your Mac's built-in camera or select an existing image from your files or the internet.

Let's say you're taking notes on a recipe and want to include a picture of the finished dish. With the image insertion feature, you can easily add a mouthwatering photo to your note, making it more visually appealing and accessible.

- ## **Organizing and Sharing Your Notes**

Once you've created your notes, the Notes app provides powerful organizational tools to help you stay on top of your work. Using keywords or handwritten text recognition, you can create

macOS Sonoma User's Guide

folders, add tags, and search for specific content within your notes.

Furthermore, with iCloud sync, your notes are automatically synced across all your Apple devices, ensuring you can access and update them from anywhere. You can also share your notes with others, collaborate in real-time, and even lock your notes with a password for added security.

Use Checklists and Tables for Better Organization

Launch the Note app by clicking on its icon in the Dock or by using Spotlight (Command + Space) to search for it. Once the app opens, you can create a new note by clicking the "New Note" button or using the keyboard shortcut Command + N.

- **Creating and Utilizing Checklists**

Checklists are a simple yet effective way to organize tasks, errands, or any items that need to be tracked or completed. The Note app in macOS

Sonoma makes creating and managing checklists within your notes incredibly easy.

To create a checklist, click the "Checklist" icon in the toolbar or use the keyboard shortcut Command + Option + L. It will insert a new checklist item within your note, complete with a checkbox. You can add as many items as you need by pressing Enter after each one.

Let's say you're planning a weekend getaway. You can create a checklist within your notes to keep track of all the tasks you need to complete, such as packing your luggage, booking accommodations, and arranging transportation. As you complete each task, check the corresponding box for a satisfying sense of accomplishment.

- **Organizing Information with Tables**

Tables are another powerful organizational tool in the Note app, allowing you to present data in a structured and visually appealing manner. Whether creating a schedule, tracking expenses, or organizing research data, tables can help you keep everything neatly organized and easy to reference.

To insert a table into your note, click the **"Table"** icon in the toolbar or use the keyboard shortcut Command + Option + T. You can customize the number of rows and columns to suit your needs. Once the table is created, you can easily add or edit content by clicking within the individual cells.

Imagine you're a student taking notes in a biology class. You can create a table to organize the species, their characteristics, and examples in your notes. It makes your notes more visually appealing and makes studying and referencing the information more accessible.

- **Combining Checklists and Tables**

While checklists and tables are powerful organizational tools, combining them can take your note-taking game to the next level. You can create highly structured and versatile note-taking layouts by integrating checklists within table cells.

For instance, if you're a project manager, you can create a table with columns for tasks, deadlines, and team members. You can insert a checklist within each task cell to break the task into smaller, actionable steps. This way, you can track the project's overall progress while monitoring the completion of individual tasks and subtasks.

Share Notes with Others

Launch the Note app and open the note you wish to share. Once the note is open, you'll find the "Share" icon in the toolbar, or you can use the keyboard shortcut Command + Shift + S.

- **Sharing via Email or Messages**

One of the most straightforward ways to share a note is through email or Apple's Messages app. When you click the "Share" icon, you'll see options to share the note via Mail or Messages. Select the desired option, and a new window will open, allowing you to enter the recipient's email address or select a contact from your iMessage app.

Let's say you're collaborating with a classmate on a research paper. You can easily share your notes by selecting the "Mail" option, entering your classmate's email address, and sending the note directly to them. This way, they can review your notes, make additions or corrections, and send the updated version back to you, streamlining the collaborative process.

- **Sharing via AirDrop**

If you're near the person you want to share your notes with, AirDrop is a convenient option. When you click on the "Share" icon, you'll see the AirDrop option. Select it, and a list of nearby devices will appear. Choose the device you want to share the note with, and it will be transferred seamlessly.

Imagine you're meeting with your team and need to share your notes with a colleague sitting across the table. Instead of emailing or messaging the note, you can use AirDrop to transfer it instantly. This way, your colleague can review the notes in real-time, ensuring everyone is on the same page.

- **Sharing via Collaboration Link**

One of the most powerful features of the Note app in macOS Sonoma is the ability to share a collaboration link. It allows multiple people to view and edit the same note simultaneously, fostering real-time collaboration and ensuring everyone works with the most up-to-date information.

To share a collaboration link, click the **"Share"** icon and select **"Share Options."** You can enable **"Collaborate"** and copy the generated link from there. You can then share this link with your collaborators via email, a messaging app, or other preferred method.

Let's say you're part of a team working on a marketing campaign. By sharing a collaboration link for your notes, everyone on the team can access and edit the notes in real-time. This way, you can brainstorm ideas, assign tasks, and track progress seamlessly, ensuring the entire team is always on the same page.

Search For Specific Notes

To access the search feature in the Notes app, launch the app and look for the search bar at the top of the window. You can also use the keyboard shortcut Command + F to instantly bring the search bar into focus.

- **Searching by Keyword**

The most straightforward way to search for a specific note is by entering a keyword or phrase that you know is contained within the note. The Notes app will dynamically filter your notes as you type, displaying only those that match your search query.

Let's say you're a student and need to find your notes on the American Revolution. Type "American

Revolution" into the search bar, and the Notes app will present you with all the notes containing those words, making locating the information you need easy.

- **Searching by Date**

In addition to searching by keyword, the Notes app in macOS Sonoma also allows you to search for notes based on their creation or modification dates. It can be helpful when finding a note you worked on recently or during a specific time.

To search by date, click on the "Filter" button in the search bar and select either "Creation Date" or "Modification Date." You can then specify a date range or choose from preset options like "Today," "This Week," or "This Month."

Imagine you're a project manager and need to review the notes you took during a client meeting last week. Click on the "Filter" button, select "Creation Date," and choose "Last Week" from the options. The Notes app will display all the notes you created during that period, making it easy to find the specific note you want.

- **Searching by Tag or Folder**

Suppose you've organized your notes using tags or folders. In that case, the Notes app in macOS Sonoma allows you to search within those categories; this can be helpful when finding a note related to a particular project or topic.

To search by tag or folder, click on the desired tag or folder in the sidebar and then use the search bar to enter your keyword or phrase. The search will be limited to the notes within that specific tag or folder, making it easier to find what you're looking for.

Let's say you're a writer working on multiple book projects. You've organized your notes using tags for each book. To find a specific note related to your latest novel, click on the corresponding book tag in the sidebar. Then, search for keywords or phrases relevant to that note. The search results will only include notes tagged with that specific book, streamlining your workflow and saving you valuable time.

CHAPTER TEN

Send and Receive Emails

The Mail app in macOS Sonoma is your gateway to email messaging. You can find it conveniently located in the Dock or by searching for it using Spotlight. Once opened, you'll be greeted by a sleek, modern interface that simplifies your email experience.

Setting Up Your Email Accounts

Before you can start sending and receiving emails, you'll need to add your email accounts to the Mail app. macOS Sonoma supports a wide range of email services, including popular ones like Gmail, Yahoo, and Outlook, as well as custom email accounts provided by your workplace or internet service provider.

To set up a new email account, click on the **"Mail" menu** in the top left corner of your screen and select **"Add Account."** Follow the prompts to enter your email address and password, and the Mail app will automatically configure your necessary settings.

macOS Sonoma offers multiple ways to access the Mail app and manage your emails. In addition to the traditional desktop application, you can also take advantage of the Mail app on your iPhone or iPad, thanks to the seamless integration of Apple's ecosystem. It means you can stay connected and respond to essential emails no matter where or what device you're using.

- **Composing and Sending Emails**

With your email accounts, you can start composing and sending messages. To create a new email, click on the "New Message" button in the top left corner of the Mail app or use the keyboard shortcut "Command + N."

The compose window will open, allowing you to enter the recipient's email address, a subject line, and the body of your message. macOS Sonoma's intelligent suggestions will assist you in quickly adding contacts from your address book or even proposing subject lines based on the content of your email.

One of the standout features of macOS Sonoma's Mail app is its ability to suggest relevant information and attachments based on the context of your email. For example, suppose you're discussing a meeting in your email. In that case, the Mail app may suggest adding a calendar invitation or attaching relevant documents from your recent work. This intelligent assistance saves time and streamlines your email workflow.

- **Receiving and Managing Emails**

Incoming emails in the Mail app are organized into various inboxes, making prioritising and responding to messages easy. macOS Sonoma's advanced filtering and search capabilities ensure you never miss an important email, even in the busiest inboxes.

Imagine you're working on a project with a team and need to locate all emails related to that project quickly. With macOS Sonoma's search functionality, you can type in a keyword or the project name, and the Mail app will instantly surface all relevant emails, attachments, and conversations, saving you valuable time and effort.

macOS Sonoma User's Guide

Create and Organize Multiple Email

Accounts

To add a new email account, click on the **"Mail"** menu in the top left corner of your screen and select **"Add Account."** It will launch a straightforward setup wizard to guide you through the process.

Whether using a popular email service like Gmail, Yahoo, or Outlook or a custom email account provided by your workplace or internet service provider, the Mail app supports a wide range of email services. Enter your email address and password, and the app will automatically configure your settings.

One of the significant advantages of macOS Sonoma is the seamless integration of the Mail app across all your Apple devices. Whether you're working on your Mac, checking emails on your iPhone, or catching up on your iPad, your email accounts and their respective settings will be synchronized, ensuring a consistent and cohesive experience no matter where you access your emails.

- **Customizing Email Accounts**

Once your accounts are set up, macOS Sonoma offers many customization options to tailor your email experience to your specific needs. You can adjust preferences such as display settings, notifications, and signature formats for each account, ensuring your professional and personal emails maintain their identities.

A standout feature in macOS Sonoma's Mail app is creating custom and smart mailboxes. Custom mailboxes allow you to organize your emails based on your preferred criteria, such as project names, client names, or specific labels. Smart mailboxes take this further by automatically updating their contents based on predefined rules, ensuring your emails are always sorted and easily accessible.

macOS Sonoma User's Guide

Manage Your Inbox, Including Folders and Labels

Folders are a fundamental organizational tool in macOS Sonoma's Mail app. They allow you to categorize your emails based on specific criteria, such as projects, clients, or personal interests. To create a new folder, right-click the desired mailbox in the sidebar and select "New Mailbox."

You can customize the folder's name and location, making it easy to find and access your emails when needed. Additionally, you can create nested folders within existing ones, enabling you to establish a hierarchical structure that suits your organizational needs.

Any changes you make to your folder structure on your Mac will automatically sync with your iPhone or iPad, ensuring that your organizational system remains consistent no matter where you access your emails.

- **Utilizing Labels**

While folders are excellent for broad categorization, labels offer a more granular approach to email organization. With macOS Sonoma's Mail app, you can assign labels to individual emails, quickly identifying and filtering messages based on specific criteria, such as importance, project status, or follow-up actions required.

A unique feature in macOS Sonoma's Mail app is creating smart mailboxes based on label filters. These dynamic mailboxes automatically populate emails matching your specified label criteria, ensuring you never miss an important message or task.

Imagine you're working on multiple projects simultaneously, each with its deadlines and priorities. By assigning labels such as "Urgent," "High Priority," or "Follow Up," you can quickly identify and prioritize the most pressing emails, ensuring that critical tasks are addressed promptly.

macOS Sonoma User's Guide

- **Combining Folders and Labels**

While folders and labels can be powerful organizational tools, their true potential is realized in tandem. Combining these two features allows you to create a highly customized and efficient email management system tailored to your needs.

For example, you could create a folder for a particular client or project and then use labels to further categorize emails within that folder based on their status or priority. This approach allows you to maintain a clear overview of your email correspondence while still being able to locate and act on specific messages when needed quickly.

Compose and Format Emails

Creating a new email in macOS Sonoma's Mail app is seamless. Click on the **"New Message"** button in the top left corner of the app or use the keyboard shortcut "Command + N." It will open a clean, distraction-free compose window, allowing you to focus solely on crafting your message.

With the Mail app's intelligent suggestions, as you begin typing, the app will recommend relevant contacts and email addresses and even suggest subject lines based on the content of your message, streamlining the composition process and saving you valuable time.

With macOS Sonoma's seamless integration across Apple devices, you can easily pick up where you left off when composing emails. Start drafting an email on your Mac, and you can continue editing or sending it from your iPhone or iPad, ensuring a consistent and uninterrupted workflow no matter where you are or which device you're using.

- **Formatting and Styling**

Once you've crafted the perfect message, macOS Sonoma's Mail app offers a range of formatting and styling options to give your emails a polished and professional appearance. The intuitive formatting toolbar allows you to adjust font styles, sizes, and colors and apply bold, italic, or underlined formatting with just a few clicks.

The Mail app supports rich text formatting. It means you can effortlessly incorporate tables, images, and even inline code snippets directly into your emails, making it easier to share complex information or showcase your work visually appealing and organized. Imagine you're collaborating with a team on a coding project. With macOS Sonoma's Mail app, you can share code snippets and include syntax highlighting directly in your emails; this ensures that your colleagues can quickly review and understand the code without needing separate attachments or tools.

- **Attachments and Email Signatures**

No email composition experience would be complete without the ability to attach files and include personalized email signatures. macOS Sonoma's Mail app makes it easy to add attachments by simply dragging and dropping files directly into the compose window or using the dedicated attachment button.

Email signatures are another powerful tool for adding a professional touch to your messages. The Mail app allows you to create and customize multiple signatures, including your contact information, company logo, and personalized quotes or taglines. These signatures can be easily applied to new emails or set as the default for specific email accounts.

Create and Manage Events

The Calendar app is conveniently located in the Applications folder on your Mac. You can still access it through various shortcuts. Click on the Calendar icon in the Dock or use Spotlight Search (Command + Space) to launch the app quickly. For added convenience, you can set up a customizable menu bar icon or use the built-in calendar widget in the Notification Center.

macOS Sonoma User's Guide

- **Creating Events**

In macOS Sonoma, creating events has never been easier. With a streamlined interface and intuitive controls, you can quickly add appointments, meetings, or reminders to your calendar. Here's how:

Open the Calendar app and navigate to the desired date or week view.

Double-click on the specific time slot or day you want to create an event.

A new event window will appear, prompting you to enter the title, location, and time details.

Optionally, you can add details such as notes, attachments, or invitees.

Once you've entered all the necessary information, click the "Save" button to add the event to your calendar.

- **Managing Events**

The Calendar app on macOS Sonoma offers a variety of features to help you manage your events efficiently. With a few clicks, you can:

Edit event details: Double-click on an existing event to modify its title, time, location, or other information.

Reschedule events: Drag and drop events to a different date or time slot to quickly reschedule them.

Set reminders: Enable reminders for important events to ensure you never miss a deadline or appointment.

Share events: Invite others to your events by sharing the calendar link or sending email invitations.

View multiple calendars: Integrate calendars from different accounts (e.g., iCloud, Google, Exchange) to manage your personal and work schedules seamlessly.

macOS Sonoma User's Guide

Set Reminders for Events

Access the Calendar app on your Mac. There are several convenient ways to do this:

Click on the Calendar icon in the Dock.

Use Spotlight Search (Command + Space) and type "Calendar" to launch the app.

Access the Calendar app through the menu bar if you've added it as a menu bar item.

Use the built-in calendar widget in the Notification Center.

- **Setting Reminders for Events**

Once you've opened the Calendar app, setting reminders is a breeze. Here's how:

Double-click on an existing event or create a new event by clicking on the desired date and time slot.

In the event details window, click on the "Reminder" section.

Select the desired reminder time from the pre-set options (e.g., 5 minutes before, 1 hour before, one day before).

Click the "Custom" option to set a specific reminder time.

If you'd like to receive multiple reminders for the same event, click on the "Add Reminder" button and follow the same process.

Once you've set your desired reminders, click "Save" to apply the changes to the event.

- **Managing Reminders**

The Calendar app on macOS Sonoma offers a variety of options to manage your reminders effectively:

Edit existing reminders: Double-click on an event and adjust the reminder time or add additional reminders as needed.

Dismiss reminders: When a reminder appears, you can dismiss it or snooze it for a later time.

Customize reminder settings: Adjust the default settings, such as sound and notification styles, to suit your preferences.

View upcoming reminders: Check the Notification Center or the Calendar app's Today view for a list of forthcoming reminders.

Share Calendars with Others

Head to the Calendar app on your Mac. There are several convenient ways to do this:

Click on the Calendar icon in the Dock.

Use Spotlight Search (Command + Space) and type "Calendar" to launch the app.

Access the Calendar app through the menu bar if you've added it as a menu bar item.

Use the built-in calendar widget in the Notification Center.

- **Sharing Your Calendar**

Once you've opened the Calendar app, sharing your calendar with others is straightforward. Here's how:

In the Calendar app, select the calendar you wish to share from the list on the left-hand side.

Click on the "Share" button in the top right corner of the app window.

A sharing window will appear, presenting you with various sharing options.

To share your calendar with specific individuals, click the "Add Person" button and enter their email addresses.

Alternatively, you can share your calendar via a public link by clicking the "Copy Link" option.

Customize the sharing permissions by selecting whether you want to grant view-only access or allow others to edit your calendar.

Once you've selected, click "Share" to finalize the process.

View Your Calendar in Different Ways

Opening the Calendar app and switching between different calendar views is a breeze. Here's how:

Day View: This view displays your events in a detailed hourly format for a single day. To access the Day View, click the "Day" button in the top left corner of the app window or select the desired date from the mini-calendar on the left-hand side.

Week View: This view provides a comprehensive overview of your events for the entire week. To access the Week View, click the "Week" button in the top left corner of the app window.

Month View: This view offers a high-level overview of your events for the entire month. To access the Month View, click the "Month" button in the top left corner of the app window.

Year View: For a broader perspective, you can switch to the Year View by clicking the "Year" button in the top left corner. This view displays your events throughout the year, allowing you to identify patterns and plan.

- **Customizing Your View**

The Calendar app on macOS Sonoma offers a variety of options to customize your calendar views for optimal convenience and productivity:

Adjust the time scale: Use the slider in the top right corner to zoom in or out, adjusting the time scale to suit your preferences.

Hide or show calendars: Toggle specific calendars on or off to declutter your view and focus on the most relevant events.

Change the color scheme: Customize the color scheme of your calendars to distinguish between different types of events or accounts.

Adjust the start of the week: Set your preferred day as the start of the week to align with your personal or professional schedule.

Subscribe to Other Calendars

Launching the Calendar app and subscribing to other calendars is a straightforward process. Here's how:

In the Calendar app, click **"File"** in the menu bar, then select **"New Calendar Subscription."**

A window will appear, prompting you to enter the calendar's subscription URL or Webcal link.

You can find these URLs or links from various sources, such as websites, online calendars, or shared calendar links from colleagues or organizations.

After entering the URL or link, click **"Subscribe"** to add the calendar to your list.

Optionally, you can customize the calendar's name, color, and other settings to suit your preferences.

The subscribed calendar will now appear in your calendar list and seamlessly integrate with your existing calendars.

CHAPTER ELEVEN

Import Photos from Your Camera or Phone

You'll primarily use the Photos app- Apple's robust photo management solution to import photos from your camera or phone to your Mac running macOS Sonoma. This application is deeply integrated into the macOS experience, making it a breeze to import, organize, and edit your photo library.

You can access the Photos app in several ways:

Spotlight Search: Press Command + Spacebar to open Spotlight, then type "Photos" and press Return.

Launchpad: Click the Launchpad icon in the Dock, then find and click the Photos app icon.

Dock: If you've previously opened Photos, its icon may be in your Dock for quick access.

Finder: Navigate to Applications > Photos in the Finder window.

Once you've launched Photos, you're ready to begin importing your precious memories.

- **Importing from a Camera**

Connecting your camera to your Mac is the quickest way to import photos directly from the device. Here's how:

Connect your camera to your Mac's USB port using the appropriate cable.

Please turn on your camera and set it to the correct mode for transferring files.

macOS Sonoma User's Guide

In the Photos app, your camera is listed in the sidebar under **"Import."**

Click on your camera's name to view its contents in the main Photos window.

Select the photos you want to import by clicking the checkbox at the window's top-left. Or, click **"Import All New Photos"** to grab everything.

Optionally, you can choose which album to import the photos into and whether to delete the imported photos from your camera.

Click "Import" to transfer your photos to your Mac's photo library.

As your photos import, Photos will keep you updated with a progress bar and estimated time remaining. Once complete, your photos will be safely stored on your Mac, ready for editing, sharing, or simply revisiting cherished memories.

- **Importing from an iPhone or iPad**

In our mobile-centric world, many photos live on our iPhones and iPads. Fortunately, macOS Sonoma and the Photos app make it a breeze to wirelessly import photos from these devices, with no cables required. Here's how:

Ensure your iPhone or iPad is connected to your Mac's Wi-Fi network.

Open the Photos app on your Mac.

Look for the "Import" section in the sidebar and click the **"Import"** button.

Select your iOS device from the list of available sources.

Enter your device's unlock code when prompted to grant your Mac access.

You'll now see all the photos and videos in the main Photos window on your device.

Select the items you wish to import or click **"Import All New Items"** to grab everything new since your last import.

Click "Import" to begin the wireless transfer.

As your photos and videos go from your iOS device to your Mac's photo library, you can watch their progress and see an estimate of the remaining time. Wireless transfers are slower than direct cable connections, but the convenience is unbeatable.

- **The New Continuity Camera**

One of the standout new features in macOS Sonoma is the Continuity Camera, which allows you to seamlessly import photos and videos from your iPhone to your Mac with just a few taps.

To use Continuity Camera, bring your iPhone near your Mac. At the same time, you have an app like Notes, Messages, or Mail open. Your Mac will automatically detect the proximity of your iPhone's camera and allow you to insert a photo or video.

Just tap the Continuity Camera button, frame your shot or record your video, then tap **"Keep"** to send it straight to your Mac. It's an effortless way to enhance documents, messages, and more with visual media from your iPhone's impressive camera system.

Organize Photos into Albums and Moments

Albums are the backbone of any well-organized photo library, allowing you to group images based on events, themes, people, or any criteria you choose. Here's how to create and populate albums in the Photos app:

In the sidebar, click the **"+" button** below "Albums."

Select "**New Album**" and give it a descriptive name, like "Summer Vacation 2023."

Drag and drop photos from your library into the new album.

Alternatively, select the pictures and click the "+" button at the top, then choose **"Create Album from Selection."**

With albums created, you can further organize by:

Reordering photos within an album by drag-and-drop.

Adding titles and descriptions to give albums more context.

Sharing entire albums via link, email, or social networks.

Enabling iCloud Photos to sync albums across all your Apple devices.

As your library grows, revisiting and adjusting your album structure keeps your collection tidy and easily navigable.

- **Utilizing Moments**

While albums are a fantastic manual organization tool, macOS Sonoma's Photos app leverages advanced algorithms to automatically group your pictures into "Moments" based on time and location data. This intelligent approach surfaces related shots in tidy clusters, saving you hours of sorting time.

To access Moments, click the "Moments" tab at the top of the Photos window. Here, you'll see thumbnails of your photo moments, with larger thumbnails representing more images in that group.

Double-clicking a Moment will display all its photos, neatly arranged by time and place. You can scroll through these images vertically or use the "Moment" button in the top-left to cycle through each moment.

One of Moments' most impressive features is the ability to detect visual similarities across your library and automatically cluster related photos together. For example, all your images from a weekend camping trip will be grouped into their Moment.

If a moment ends up containing unrelated shots, you can refine it further if you:

Select and press "Shift-Command-N" to create a new moment from the selection.

Drag out images to move them to other moments.

Use smart albums and filtering to isolate photos from specific locations or periods.

With intelligent assistance from Moments and your discerning eye for organization, you'll have an impeccably curated photo library to cherish for years.

- **The "On My Mac" Folder**

Before we wrap up, here is a brief word about the "On My Mac" folder in the Photos sidebar. It is an exceptional location where Photos stores all your fully imported images and videos that aren't already in iCloud.

While you can't directly reorganize content within this folder, knowing its purpose helps you understand your library's structure. As you create albums and moments, rest assured that your

Perry Hoover

original files remain neatly stored in the "On My Mac" repository.

Edit Photos with Basic Tools

Launch the Photos app from your Dock, Launchpad, or Spotlight search to get started editing your photos. Once open, navigate to the image you wish to enhance, then click the "Edit" button in the top toolbar or press Return on your keyboard.

It will open the Edit pane, revealing various editing tools tailored to help you craft your photographic vision. The tools are divided into three sections - Adjust, Filters, and Crop - allowing you to make global adjustments, apply stylistic effects, and perfect your framing with just a few clicks.

Let's explore some of the standout features in each section.

- ## The Adjust Tools

Often, only minor tweaks are needed to take a photo from good to great. The Adjust tools give you precise control over the core aspects of your image:

Light: Adjust exposure, brightness, highlights, shadows, and more to ensure proper lighting and rich detail.

Color: Fine-tune color temperature, saturation, vibrancy, and even specific color ranges like skin tones.

Black & White: Convert to monochrome with optional color filters for a timeless look.

Sharpen/Noise Reduction: Bring crispness to your shots or smooth away unwanted graininess.

Definitions: Clarify edges and enhance local contrast for more "pop."

Vignette: Add a subtle darkened border to help focus the viewer's eye.

Perry Hoover

The app generates non-destructive edits as you adjust, ensuring your original photo remains unaltered. You can compare your adjustments against the original by clicking the backslash key or using automatic suggestions from the Magic Wand tool.

- **Creative Filter Effects**

For those times when subtlety is overrated, the Filters section invites you to get creative and transform your image with an array of eye-catching effects:

Vivid: Intensify colors for a vibrant, high-contrast look.

Dramatic: Give your scene a cinematic, high-drama appearance.

Silvertone: Bathe your photo in cool, silvery tones for a modern vibe.

Noir: Channel your inner film noir with a high-contrast, gritty black-and-white rendition.

And many more stylistic filters to explore.

macOS Sonoma User's Guide

The filters are fully adjustable, allowing you to dial in your desired look precisely. Additionally, you can stack multiple filters together for truly unique, layered effects.

- **Precise Cropping and Straightening**

Sometimes, the difference between a good photo and a great one lies in its framing and perspective. The Crop tool helps you achieve visual perfection:

Manually drag the corners to crop out distractions and recompose your subject.

Constrain to standard aspect ratios like 16:9 or square format.

Use the Straighten tool to correct skewed horizons and angled shots.

Rotate or flip your image as needed for the desired orientation.

The crop overlay provides a real-time preview of your adjustments. At the same time, visual guides

Share Photos with Others

No matter where you are in the Photos app, you'll always have access to robust sharing capabilities through the Share menu. Select one or more photos you wish to share, then click the Share button in the top toolbar (or press the keyboard shortcut Shift-Command-M).

It will open the Share pane, presenting you with an array of destinations to send your photos. With a click, you can instantly share via AirDrop Messages, Mail, Notes, or Reminders. For broader distribution, use the options to post directly to social media platforms like Facebook, Flickr, Twitter, and more.

- **Refining Your Shared Photos**

Before firing off your photos, the Share pane allows you to make final preparations to ensure your shared images have maximum impact:

Resize the shared versions to economize file size while preserving quality.

Optionally include location data from when/where the photos were taken.

Add a caption or comment to provide context and your personal touch.

Mark up images directly in the Share pane using the annotation tools.

These minor refinements go a long way toward creating truly memorable and meaningful shares.

- **Creating Shared Albums**

Shared Albums offer the perfect solution for sharing a collection of photos - like from a wedding, vacation, or other special event. These allow you to upload images to iCloud, which are accessible to anyone you invite.

To create a new Shared Album:

Click the "+" button beneath Shared Albums in the Photos sidebar.

Name your album and add a description if desired.

Choose whether to make the album public (viewable by anyone) or private (requires an invite).

Define additional sharing options like allowing subscribers to post their photos.

Click "Create" to generate a shareable link for your album.

Now, send that link to friends and family members. Once subscribed, they can view all current and newly added photos in the album from any of their Apple devices. You can also allow subscribers to add pictures and videos, creating a collaborative album that comprehensively captures the entire experience.

- **Mail Drop for Supersized Sharing**

While convenient, sharing photos via email does have its limitations - many email servers put strict caps on how much data you can send and receive in a single message; this is where macOS Sonoma's handy **Mail Drop** feature comes into play.

When you attempt to attach large photos to an email draft, Photos will automatically upload the full-resolution versions to iCloud and include lightweight placeholders in the message instead. The recipients can then download the originals at their convenience.

This intelligent data management lets you share prolific amounts of photos without worrying about file size limitations. Whether sharing entire shoot galleries with clients or sending high-res memories to loved ones, Mail Drop ensures your precious shots make it to their destination with ease.

Tip: To check your available iCloud storage or purchase more if needed, click on the Apple logo > System Settings > Apple ID.

Create Slideshows and Presentations

Launch Photos from your Dock, Launchpad, or using Spotlight search. Select the photos you wish to include in your slideshow. Click the "Slideshow" button in the toolbar (or press Shift-Command-P).

Alternatively, you can create a new Album or Smart Album specifically for your slideshow content and then launch the slideshow from there.

Once in Slideshow mode, prepare to be whisked away on a visually captivating journey through your most treasured photographic tales.

- **Customizing Your Slideshow**

While the default slideshow settings are serviceable, true visual storytellers will want to leverage the wealth of customization tools at their fingertips. Click the "Options" button to reveal an array of powerful yet user-friendly controls:

Transitions: Choose from stylish slide transitions like Dissolve, Wipe, and magical 3D cube effects.

Theme: Apply unified visual themes with complementary fonts and colors for titles and captions.

Music: Set the mood by selecting an audio track from your music library or iTunes to accompany your slideshow.

Beyond these global settings, you can further refine each slide individually:

Titles: Add descriptive titles to provide context for each image or scene.

Captions: Include extended captions detailing locations, subjects, or snippets of relevant backstory.

Duration: Precisely control how long each slide appears on the screen before transitioning.

This fine-grained control lcts you carefully pace and choreograph your visual narrative for maximum impact and engagement.

- **Embellishing with Editing Tools**

When you think your slideshow couldn't be more compelling, Photos enables you to edit images on the fly without pre-processing in an external editor.

While in Slideshow mode, double-click any slide to enter an intuitive editing workspace.

You'll find all the powerful adjustment tools and filters we explored in our photo editing tutorial here. Tweak exposure and color, apply stylized effects, and perform light cropping or straightening as needed. These live edits are temporary, leaving your original photo untouched while allowing your slideshows to shine with production-level polish.

- **Advanced Slideshow Themes**

Beyond the tried-and-true customization options, macOS Sonoma introduces a fresh dimension to your slideshows: advanced, cinema-inspired themes. With evocative names like "Vintage Prints" and "Opsis," these themes combine tastefully animated layouts, beautiful title fonts, and artfully orchestrated motion effects.

Select one of these themes from the Options menu to see your photos dynamically arranged in that theme's custom layout. You'll be amazed at how professional and aesthetically refined your slideshow appears with minimal effort on your part.

These themes are ideal for creating presentations to share with friends, family, colleagues - or even paid clients if you're an aspiring photographer looking to showcase your portfolio in a truly cinematic fashion.

- **Recording, Exporting, and Sharing Your Slideshow**

Once you've meticulously assembled and fine-tuned your visual journey, you'll want to share it with the world. Photos provide several straightforward methods for this:

Export to Video File: Save your slideshow as a video file optimized for sharing and playback on any device.

Record to Disk: Capture your whole slideshow experience - complete with titles, transitions, and music - as a seamless video.

AirPlay Mirroring: Effortlessly beam your slideshow to an Apple TV for big-screen viewing.

Share Options: Send your exported video via Mail, Messages, AirDrop, social media, and more.

With these robust multimedia capabilities at your fingertips, transforming personal photo collections into dazzling cinematic experiences has never been more accessible. So let your inner storyteller shine and captivate loved ones and broader audiences with the engaging narrative magic of Photos slideshows on macOS Sonoma.

- **And If You Need Professional-Grade Editing**

While the Photos app packs an impressive array of basic editing and slideshow creation tools, you may eventually outgrow its consumer-focused feature set. Look no further than Apple's industry-leading apps, Final Cut Pro and Motion, for professional-grade photo editing, color grading, and video production capabilities.

Final Cut Pro provides an intense and precise editing environment tailored for filmmakers, allowing for multi-cam editing, advanced color correction, and audio work that puts you in the editor's chair of your professional studio.

Meanwhile, Motion takes graphics, titles, and motion effects to new heights with robust particle systems, mind-bending 3D animation, and ultra-realistic lighting effects.

Using Quick Look

Quick Look is one of those beautifully unobtrusive tools that blends seamlessly into the macOS experience. You can summon its X-ray vision from virtually anywhere in the Finder:

While browsing folders, select a file and press the Space bar.

Use the keyboard shortcut Command-Y with a file selected.

Control-click or right-click on a file and choose "Quick Look" from the contextual menu.

When you trigger Quick Look, the Finder window will dim behind a sleek, borderless overlay displaying the selected file's contents front and center.

- **Navigating Quick Look's Feature Set**

While viewing simplicity itself, Quick Look offers an impressive array of tools to help you get the most out of your previews. Here are some standout features to explore:

Documents and PDFs

Browse between pages using the arrow keys, trackpad, or scroll gesture.

Enable Thumbnails for a film-strip overview of all pages.

Choose View > Show Sidebar for a table of contents or page thumbnails.

Search within the document by pressing Command-F.

Images

Zoom in/out using the standard pinch and scroll gestures.

View image metadata like EXIF information with the Inspector (Control-Command-I).

Browse galleries of multiple images using the Left/Right arrow keys.

Video and Audio

Press Space to pause/resume playback.

Use the volume keys to adjust audio levels.

Take Quick Look full-screen for maximum immersion.

With this handy toolset, Quick Look transforms from a simple file previewer into an interactive workspace for lightweight file inspection and triage.

- **Quick Actions for Rapid File Processing**

Quick Actions feature is one of Quick Look's powerful yet underutilized capabilities. With a compatible file open for preview, click the "Actions" button in the toolbar to reveal a context-sensitive menu of actions you can take on that file type.

For example, when previewing an image with Quick Look, you may see actions for editing, markup, rotation, and even screen sharing via Messages or Mail. Quick Actions might offer options to create a PDF, mark up annotations, or run optical character recognition when previewing a document.

These quick actions allow you to rapidly process files and perform everyday tasks without leaving Quick Look or launching dedicated apps. It's a great productivity booster.

For developers, Quick Actions can also be extended through Automator or scripting to add custom actions tailored to your workflows.

- **A Spotlight on Quick Look's Search Powers**

While Quick Look excels at previewing known file types, it also provides a potent method for quickly triaging files when their contents or origins are uncertain. Spotlight drives this functionality, and it is macOS's built-in search engine.

Whenever you trigger Quick Look on a file Spotlight cannot identify, it will automatically perform deep content analysis to discern the nature of the file; this could involve scanning for text contents, detecting media types, decompressing archives, and more.

If Spotlight recognizes the contents, Quick Look will display the file accordingly with an icon badge indicating its type, such as "Word Document" or "Audio recording." Quick Look provides a bytes view with hexadecimal examination for files that remain stubbornly unidentified. You can even search within this bytes view by pressing Command-F.

This seamless integration of Spotlight's content intelligence makes Quick Look a versatile tool for inspecting unknown file types - perfect for sniffing out suspicious downloads or attached files from untrusted sources.

- **Quick Look: A Quintessential macOS Experience**

At its core, Quick Look exemplifies the macOS design philosophy of improving efficiency through minimalism and intuitive design. By allowing you to rapidly inspect files without interrupting your current workflow, Quick Look eliminates those nagging "Do I want to open that?" hesitations we all experience.

It streamlines so many everyday file-related tasks into a consistent, content-first interface. Preview PDFs, documents, media files, and vet downloads for safety - all with a quick tap of the Space bar. Seamless integration with Spotlight smarts and Quick Actions also adds surprising utility for power users.

CHAPTER TWELVE

Create and Edit Documents with Pages

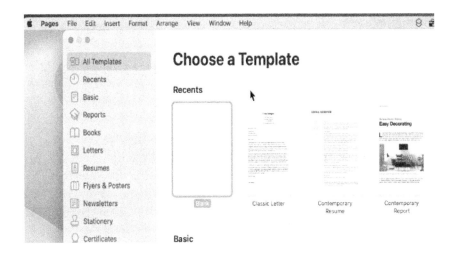

The Pages app is a word-processing tool allowing you to create beautiful documents easily. Whether you're writing a report, crafting a newsletter, or designing a poster, Pages provides a user-friendly interface and a wide range of features to help you bring your ideas to life.

- **Accessing Pages on Your Mac**

There are several ways to access the Pages app on your Mac running macOS Sonoma:

Spotlight Search: Press Command + Space Bar to open Spotlight, type "Pages," and press Enter.

Launchpad: Click the Launchpad icon in the Dock, then click the Pages icon.

Applications Folder: Go to Finder > Applications, and double-click the Pages icon.

Once you've launched Pages, you'll be greeted with a clean interface and various templates, ranging from blank documents to pre-designed layouts for reports, letters, and more.

- **Creating a New Document**

To begin creating a new document, click the "New Document" button in the bottom-left corner of the

macOS Sonoma User's Guide

Pages window. You'll be presented with a gallery of templates designed for a specific purpose.

Let's say you want to create a report. Scroll through the templates until you find one labeled "Report" or something similar. Double-click on the template to open it, and you'll see a pre-formatted document with placeholder text and images.

From here, you can start customizing the document to suit your needs. Replace the placeholder text with your content, and adjust the formatting, layout, and design elements as desired.

Format Text, Including Fonts, Styles, and Colors

Formatting text is crucial to creating visually appealing and professional-looking documents in the Pages app.

- ## **Accessing Text Formatting Tools**

There are several ways to access the text formatting tools in Pages on your Mac running macOS Sonoma:

Toolbar: The Toolbar at the top of the Pages window provides quick access to commonly used formatting options, such as font styles, text alignment, and list styles.

Format Menu: Go to the Pages menu at the top of your screen and select "Format" to reveal a dropdown menu with various text formatting options.

Shortcut Menu: Right-click (or Control-click) on selected text to create a contextual menu with formatting options.

Formatting Sidebar: Click on the "View" menu and select "Show Formatting Sidebar" (or press Option + Command + F) to display a comprehensive sidebar with all text formatting controls.

macOS Sonoma User's Guide

- **Changing Fonts and Font Styles**

One of the most fundamental aspects of text formatting is choosing the right font and font style. Pages offer a vast library of built-in fonts, ranging from classic serif and sans-serif options to modern, decorative typefaces.

To change the font, select the text you want to modify, then choose the desired font from the Font dropdown menu in the Toolbar, Formatting Sidebar, or Format menu. You can also use the keyboard shortcut Command + T to access the Font menu quickly.

Once you've selected a font, you can enhance its appearance by applying various font styles, such as bold, italic, underline, or strikethrough. These options can be found in the Toolbar, Formatting Sidebar, or Format menu, or you can use the corresponding keyboard shortcuts (e.g., Command + B for bold, Command + I for italic).

- **Adjusting Text Size, Color, and Spacing**

In addition to fonts and font styles, Pages offer a range of options for adjusting text size, color, and spacing. These elements can significantly impact the overall look and readability of your document.

Select the desired text and use the Font Size dropdown menu in the Toolbar or Formatting Sidebar to change the text size. Alternatively, you can use the keyboard shortcut Command + Shift + > to increase the font size or Command + Shift + < to decrease it.

In macOS Sonoma, Pages introduces a new feature called "Dynamic Type," which allows you to create responsive text that automatically adjusts its size based on the user's preferred reading size settings. This feature can be handy for creating accessible documents or materials for various viewing environments.

To change the text color, select the text you want to modify and click the Text Color button in the

Toolbar or Formatting Sidebar. It will bring up a color palette where you can choose from a wide range of pre-defined colors or create a custom color by entering specific RGB or hex values.

Finally, you can adjust the spacing between lines of text (leading) and between individual characters (kerning) using the respective controls in the Text section of the Formatting Sidebar.

Insert Images, Tables, and Charts

- **Inserting Images**

Adding images to your Page documents can enhance their visual appeal and provide valuable context or supporting information. To insert an image, follow these steps:

Place your cursor where you want the image to appear in your document.

Click the **"Media"** button in the Toolbar or go to the Insert menu and select "Image" (or use the keyboard shortcut Command + Option + I).

Choose your desired image file from the Finder window that appears, or drag and drop the image directly into your document.

Once the image is inserted, you can resize it, apply various styles, and even wrap text around it for a polished, professional look.

- **Working with Tables**

Tables are indispensable tools for organizing and presenting data clearly and in a structured manner. Pages offer various table formatting options to help you create visually appealing and well-organized tables. Here's how to insert a table:

Position your cursor where you want the table to appear in your document.

Click the "Table" button in the Toolbar or go to the Insert menu and select "Table."

macOS Sonoma User's Guide

In the Insert Table window, specify the number of rows and columns, and click "OK."

From there, you can customize the table's appearance, including cell borders, shading, text formatting, and more, using the various options in the Table section of the Formatting Sidebar.

- **Adding Charts and Graphs**

Visualizing data through charts and graphs can make complex information more digestible and impactful. Pages provides a comprehensive charting tool that allows you to create various chart types, including bar charts, line graphs, pie charts, and more.

Place your cursor where you want the chart to appear in your document.

Click the "Chart" button in the Toolbar or go to the Insert menu and select "Chart."

Choose the desired chart type from the Insert Chart window, and click "OK."

Enter your data into the corresponding cells in the appears Chart Data Editor.

One of the standout features in macOS Sonoma's Pages app is the ability to create interactive charts that automatically update as you edit the underlying data. This feature can be beneficial for creating dynamic reports or presentations that need to reflect the latest information.

After creating your chart, you can customize its appearance by adjusting colors, labels, and other visual elements using the options in the Chart section of the Formatting Sidebar.

Collaborate on Documents with Others

Before collaborating on a document, you need to enable the collaboration feature. Here's how:

Open the document you want to collaborate on in Pages.

macOS Sonoma User's Guide

Go to the **Share menu** and select **"Collaborate with Others."**

In the Collaborate window, choose how you want to share your document:

Send a link: This option generates a secure link you can share with your collaborators via email, messaging, or other means.

Send a copy: This option creates a copy of the document you can share with your collaborators.

Click "Send" to proceed.

Once you've shared the document, your collaborators will receive an invitation to join, and you'll be able to see their edits in real-time as they make them.

- **Collaborating in Real-Time**

One of the features of collaboration in Pages is the ability to work on the same document simultaneously with your collaborators. As you and your team members make changes, you'll see their cursors moving across the document, and their edits will appear instantaneously.

To ensure a smooth collaborative experience, Pages offers a range of tools to help you communicate and coordinate your efforts:

Insert comments: You can add comments to specific document parts to provide feedback, ask questions, or share ideas with your collaborators.

View collaborator activity: The Collaborator List in the Toolbar displays the names of all participants working on the document, making it easy to see who's contributing.

Track changes: Pages automatically keep track of all revisions made to the document, allowing you to review and accept or reject changes as needed.

- **Resolving Conflicts and Maintaining Version Control**

Conflicts may arise when multiple people are working on the same document. The Pages app is designed to handle these situations gracefully, ensuring that no one's work is lost and that conflicts are resolved fairly and transparently.

Suppose two collaborators try to edit the same part of the document simultaneously. Pages will prompt them to review and resolve the conflict in that case. You can keep one version, merge the changes, or revert to a previous document version.

In macOS Sonoma, Pages introduces a new feature called **"Version History,"** which allows you to browse through the complete revision history of your document, including all changes made by collaborators. This feature can be invaluable when you need to review or reference previous versions of your work.

Share and Export Documents in Different Formats

One of the most convenient ways to share your Pages documents is through iCloud, Apple's cloud storage and syncing service. By saving your document to iCloud, you can grant access to specific individuals or share a public link that anyone can view.

Open the document you want to share in Pages.

Click on the "Collaborate" button in the Toolbar.

Select "Share" and choose whether to share with specific people or create a public link.

Follow the prompts to grant access or copy the shareable link.

Once shared, your collaborators can view and make changes to the document in real-time, making iCloud an ideal solution for collaborative projects.

- **Exporting to Other File Formats**

While Pages is designed to work seamlessly with other Apple applications, there may be times when you need to share your documents with individuals or organizations that use different software platforms. Fortunately, Pages allows you to export your documents in various formats, ensuring compatibility and accessibility.

Open the document you want to export in Pages.

Go to the "File" menu and select "Export To" (or use the keyboard shortcut Command + E).

Choose the desired file format from the available options, such as PDF, Microsoft Word, EPUB, or Plain Text.

Customize any export settings if prompted, then click "Export" to save the file in the selected format.

Exporting to different file formats can be particularly useful when sharing documents with colleagues, clients, or publishers who may have specific software requirements or preferences.

- **Sharing via Email or Cloud Storage Services**

In addition to iCloud, Pages integrates seamlessly with other popular sharing methods, such as email and cloud storage services like Dropbox, Google Drive, and OneDrive.

Open the document you want to share in Pages.

Click on the "Share" button in the Toolbar (or go to the "File" menu and select "Share").

Choose your preferred sharing method, such as "Mail" or your cloud storage service.

Follow the prompts to complete the sharing process, including adding recipients or specifying sharing settings.

By leveraging these sharing options, you can ensure that your documents reach their intended audience quickly and efficiently, regardless of their location or the tools they're using.

One of the standout features in macOS Sonoma's Pages app is the ability to share documents as interactive web pages. This feature lets you publish your content online, making it accessible to anyone with a web browser without needing specialized software or plugins. It can help create visually stunning digital portfolios, presentations, or online brochures.

Create and Edit Spreadsheets with Numbers

Numbers is Apple's sleek and user-friendly spreadsheet application that comes pre-installed on all new Macs running macOS. With an intuitive interface and robust feature set, Numbers makes crunching numbers, visualizing data, and collaborating on spreadsheets a breeze.

- **Accessing Numbers on Your Mac**

To start, open the Launchpad on your Mac and click the Numbers icon. You can also use Spotlight search by pressing Command + Space Bar, typing "Numbers" and hitting Enter.

- **Creating a New Spreadsheet**

Once Numbers is open, you have a few options to create a new spreadsheet document:

Click **"New Document"** in the bottom left of the Numbers window.

Use the keyboard shortcut Command + N.

Go to **File > New** to reveal templates you can use as a starting point.

The blank canvas allows you to build your spreadsheet from scratch or use pre-made templates for budgets, invoices, grade books, and more.

Enter and Format Data

Creating great-looking and functional spreadsheets starts with entering and formatting your data correctly. The Numbers app makes this process intuitive and efficient with its nifty data entry tools and comprehensive formatting options.

- **Accessing the Numbers App**

To start, open the Launchpad on your Mac and click the Numbers icon. You can also use Spotlight search by pressing Command+Space, typing "Numbers", and hitting Return.

- **Creating a New Spreadsheet**

Once Numbers is open, create a new blank spreadsheet by going to File > New or using the keyboard shortcut Command+N. It gives you a fresh canvas to start building your data masterpiece.

- **Entering Data**

Begin by clicking into the first cell (the intersection of a row and column) and typing your entry. Numbers automatically recognize different data types like numbers, dates, times, and currencies as you type.

You can use the arrow keys and tab buttons to move to the next cell or click the target cell with your mouse. The intelligent autocomplete will suggest matching entries from existing data as you type for extra speed.

- **Basic Formatting**

Once you've entered some initial data, it's time to apply formatting to make it look clean and polished. Select the cells you want to format, then use the formatting tools in the toolbar:

Font style, size, and color

Cell fill color

Number format (currency, percentage, decimal places, etc.)

Text formatting like bold, italic, underline

Horizontal and vertical alignment

- **Advanced Formatting with Styles**

Try applying a pre-made style from the Styles pane for more intricate formatting. These comprehensive styles can transform the look of your entire sheet with just one click.

Go to **View > Show Styles Drawer** or click the **Styles button** in the toolbar to access Styles. Browse the various styles and preview how they will look on your data before applying.

- **Conditional Formatting**

You can also apply conditional formatting rules to change how cells are formatted automatically based on their values. For example, make all negative numbers appear in red or highlight the highest value in green.

Select the cells you want the rule to apply, then go to **Format > Conditional Formatting.** Set the criteria and formatting, then click Done.

- **Text Wrapping and Merging**

Two more helpful formatting tricks are text wrapping and cell merging. Enable text wrapping to allow long entries to display on multiple lines within the cell instead of overflowing. To merge several neighboring cells into one, select them and click the Merge button.

Use Formulas and Functions for

Calculations

Crunching numbers and deriving insights are the core purposes of any spreadsheet app, and the Numbers app in macOS Sonoma provides powerful tools to do just that through formulas and functions.

- **Understanding Formulas**

A formula is an equation that performs operations on values in your spreadsheet. They begin with an equal sign (=) followed by references to cells, arithmetic operators, functions, and more.

For example, to add the values in cells A1 and B1, you'd enter =A1+B1.

- **Basic Math Operations**

Numbers support all the basic arithmetic operators:

Addition

Subtraction

Multiplication/Division

You can combine multiple operations in a single formula following the standard order of operations.

- **Using Cell References**

Where formulas shine is utilizing cell references instead of hardcoded values. It allows you to build dynamic calculations that update automatically when the referenced cells change.

For example, =A1*B2 multiplies the current values in cells A1 and B2.

- **Working with Functions**

Functions are pre-built formulas that perform specific calculations like sums, averages, maximums, etc. Numbers includes an extensive library:

Statistical: AVERAGE, MAX, MIN, COUNT, etc.

Financial: PMT, FV, NPV, IRR

Logical: IF, AND, OR

Text: CONCAT, PROPER, LEN

And many more categories.

To use a function, type an equal sign followed by the function name and required arguments in parentheses.

Example: =AVERAGE(A1:A10) finds the average values in the range A1 through A10.

- **The Formula Editor**

While you can type formulas directly into cells, the Formula Editor provides a user-friendly way to construct calculations. Access it by clicking the Formula button in the toolbar.

The top displays your formula, with areas below to insert functions, operators, cell/range references, and more from drop-downs. Double-check your inputs before accepting.

- **Array Formulas**

For advanced data analysis, numbers support array formulas simultaneously calculated across entire rows or columns, not just single values.

To create an array formula, select the range for the output and enter the formula as expected, but press Control+Return instead of Return.

Let's look at an example array formula to find the highest score in a range:

=MAX(A1:A20)

If you entered this typically, it would only return the maximum value in A1:A20 in the current cell. As an array formula across A1:A20, it will populate the highest value into each cell of that range.

Create Charts and Graphs

They say a picture is worth a thousand words, and charts are how to visualize your spreadsheet data and convey insights. The Numbers app provides a comprehensive and user-friendly chart creation toolset to transform your numbers into vivid, illuminating visuals.

- **Selecting Data for Your Chart**

The first step is selecting the data range you want to visualize. Click and drag across the cells to highlight them, or click the column letter or row number to select the entire column or row.

- **Creating a New Chart**

With your data selected, click the Chart button in the toolbar or **Insert > Chart**; this opens the Chart editor sidebar.

Here you can choose from an impressive gallery of 2D and 3D chart types - bar, line, pie, scatter, bubble, and more. Numbers intelligently recommends the best visualizations based on your selected data.

- **Customizing Chart Type and Style**

Once you've selected a regular chart type that fits your data, the editing options allow you to dial in the perfect look and layout.

macOS Sonoma User's Guide

Use the Style Options pane to apply one of Numbers' modern, polished chart styles with a single click. Customize the color scheme, add chart titles and axes labels, adjust spacing and scaling, and more.

- **Interactive Chart Previews**

As you explore different customizations, Numbers provides an interactive live preview within the Chart editor. Instantly see how each adjustment impacts the overall visualization without having to confirm changes.

This intuitive preview workflow enables rapid iteration to achieve precisely the chart you have in mind for your data story.

- **Advanced Editing and Analytics**

For more advanced charting needs, click the Edit Chart Data button to modify the underlying data and calculations powering the visualization.

You can add trendlines, drop lines, error bars, and other advanced analytics directly onto the chart canvas. Numbers also supports chart animations, color coding by data value ranges, and overlaid combinations of multiple chart types.

Once your masterpiece is complete, Numbers automatically creates a linked chart object that dynamically updates when you modify data in the spreadsheet. Perfect for reports, presentations, and dashboards.

Share and Export Spreadsheets in Different Formats

Once you've put the finishing touches on your Numbers spreadsheet, it's time to share your work with others or save it in a format for use across different platforms and applications.

- **Sharing via iCloud**

For collaborating with others in real-time, Numbers leverages iCloud to enable seamless co-editing and sharing. With your spreadsheet open, click the Share button in the toolbar and enter the email

macOS Sonoma User's Guide

addresses or names of those you'd like to grant access.

You can give recipients the ability to view the spreadsheet or make edits. Any changes will sync instantly across everyone's devices. This cloud-based collaboration is perfect for team projects, client revisions, or working remotely.

- **Exporting to Other Formats**

Sometimes, you need to save your spreadsheet in a specific file format, whether for use in another application or sharing with non-Numbers users. Numbers support exports to many popular formats:

Microsoft Excel (.xlsx)

PDF (.pdf)

CSV (.csv)

To export, go to File > Export and select your desired format. You can then attach this exported file version to emails, upload it to cloud storage, or open it in another compatible program like Microsoft Excel or Google Sheets.

- **Printing**

Numbers provides robust printing capabilities for sharing physical printed copies directly from the app. Go to **File > Print**, and use the preview pane to select your printer, paper size, orientation, and other settings like which sheets or objects to include.

You can even perform a PDF Quick Look here by clicking the PDF button before sending it to the printer. It generates a print-ready PDF preview to double-check the output.

- **Export Options**

When exporting to PDF or Excel format, the Export Options window appears with additional settings to customize your file:

macOS Sonoma User's Guide

Password Protection

Attach a password to restrict the opening or modification of the exported file.

PDF Tags

You can preserve important spreadsheet structures for PDF exports with options like formulas and comments.

Sheets to Export

Choose to export the entire spreadsheet or only specific sheet tabs.

CHAPTER THIRTEEN

Create and Edit Presentations with Keynotes

With the new macOS Sonoma update, Apple has made crafting stunning presentations with the Keynote app even more effortless. Whether you need to design slides for an upcoming meeting, conference, or classroom lecture, Keynote's intuitive interface and powerful features have you covered.

- **Accessing Keynote on Your Mac**

There are several ways to open the Keynote app on your macOS Sonoma system. The quickest route is to use Spotlight Search – press the Command+Space bar and start typing "Keynote." You can also find it in the Applications folder of your dock or use Launchpad.

- **Creating a New Presentation**

Once Keynote is open, you'll be greeted by a crisp interface and the option to choose a theme for your new presentation. Apple provides a range of modern templates to get you started, or you can select one of the blank layouts. As you scroll through the template chooser, you'll get a live preview of how your content will look with each theme applied.

Let's say you want to assemble a pitch deck for a potential investor. The Premium Office template could perfectly fit with its clean typography and corporate aesthetic. Once you've selected, click "Choose," and you'll be taken to the editing canvas.

Add Slides with Different Layouts and Content

One of the keys to crafting an engaging presentation in Keynote is utilizing a variety of slide layouts and content types. It allows you to smoothly guide your audience through your narrative while keeping things visually interesting.

- **Adding a New Slide**

The first step is inserting a new slide into your presentation. There are a few different ways to do this in Keynote. The simplest is to click the "Add Slide" button in the toolbar or use the keyboard shortcut Option+Command+N. You can also control-click anywhere on the slide navigation pane on the left and select "Add Slide" from the contextual menu.

macOS Sonoma User's Guide

- ## Choosing a Layout

Once the new slide thumbnail appears in the navigation pane, you'll want to select the layout that best suits the content you plan to include on that slide. Keynote provides countless built-in layout options accessible by clicking the **"Layout"** button or using the Layout dropdown in the toolbar.

For example, if you need to display a bulleted list and a supporting image, you could choose the **"Title & Content"** layout. Or, if you're about to unveil an impressive data visualization, the "Title & Blank" layout would allow that chart or graph to take center stage.

- ## Adding Text Content

With your desired slide layout selected, inputting your content is time. For text, click on the placeholder boxes and start typing. The inline formatting tools allow you to easily adjust styling like font, size, color, and alignment.

Expert Tip: For longer text entries, consider using Keynote's **"View"** menu to enter an Outline editing mode, which allows you to work with just the text and is free of visual distractions.

- **Incorporating Multimedia**

To give your presentations some pop, take advantage of Keynote's multimedia capabilities by embedding photos, videos, audio clips, interactive charts and more onto your slides. Drag and drop files from Finder onto the slide canvas or use the "Add" buttons in the toolbar.

You can even liven things up by including live web content. With Keynote's Web View option, you can embed entire websites, online documents, or streaming media into your slides.

- **Using Object Placeholders**

Another powerful feature of Keynote is the ability to define placeholders for objects you plan to swap in and out across multiple slide versions or presentation runs. For example, if you need to customize a particular slide deck for different client meetings, you could set up placeholders for client logos, project media, and other variable content.

To set up a placeholder, drag in the type of media you want to use as a placeholder item, then select the **"Define as Placeholder"** option from the object's contextual menu. You can then easily swap in new content whenever needed without rebuilding the entire slide.

- **Organizing with Groups and Headers**

As your presentation grows with more varied slide layouts and content, keeping things organized using Keynote's grouping capabilities is essential. You can nest multiple objects into groups, treating them as a single unit that's easy to move, copy or resize.

The software also supports adding section headers that extend across the slide navigation pane, perfect for segmenting your presentation into logical chapters or acts. Control-click on any slide thumbnail and select "Add Section Header" from the menu.

Format Text, Images, and Videos

Creating visually compelling presentations goes beyond just having solid content – you need to format and style that content to achieve maximum impact. The Keynote app in macOS Sonoma provides a powerful yet user-friendly set of formatting tools to help you do just that, whether you're working with text, images, videos or other multimedia objects.

- **Formatting Text**

For text, Keynote's formatting pane provides a rich array of accessible options with just a few clicks. You can adjust basics like font face, size, color, and styling, as well as more advanced properties such as character spacing, baseline offsets, and underline styles. The software includes built-in font libraries for specialized needs like math equations or computer code.

To efficiently format longer bodies of text, try using the Outline view to work solely with the text content. You can define heading levels, apply styling and rearrange the flow, then quickly switch back to the slide editor to see your changes applied.

- **Image Adjustments**

High-quality visuals are essential for engaging presentations, so Keynote provides plenty of tools for fine-tuning your images and graphics. With an image selected, the Format pane transforms to show adjustment options like crop, rotate, color levels, transparency and more.

You can apply stylized image filters and effects like Gaussian blurs, color monochrome, or noise textures. It allows you to artfully integrate graphics with the aesthetic of your overall presentation design.

- **Positioning and Layering**

Once the text and graphics look right, you must carefully position and layer those objects on the slide canvas. Keynote's alignment guides make it easy to position elements precisely, or you can enable the well-designed layout guides to have objects automatically snap into pleasing formations.

For complex slides, make use of the layering and grouping capabilities. You can stack objects in front or behind others, nest groups of objects within groups, and even define alpha transparency levels for fine-grained blending.

- **Multimedia Controls**

Speaking of video, Keynote provides flexible controls for incorporating multimedia like audio, movies, live video and interactive web content. You can trim and adjust playback regions, set looping behaviors, control media navigation and more. There are also options to auto-play versus click-to-play for different scenarios.

The new macOS Sonoma update includes an inline video preview for live video objects like webcam feeds to ensure proper framing and overlays before presenting. You can even set spotlight visibility and background removal options.

- **Styling Masters**

For total design control across your entire presentation, take advantage of Keynote's master slide capabilities. Here, you can define universal styling for elements like backgrounds, fonts, colors and object placeholders. Any changes made to the master will dynamically apply across all associated slides.

You can create library-customized themes and reuse them for future presentations, streamlining your workflow while maintaining design consistency.

Use Animations and Transitions

Captivating your audience relies on more than great content – you need to orchestrate that content with motion and visual energy; this is where Keynote's animation and transition capabilities shine on MacOS Sonoma. With an intuitive set of tools, you can breathe life into static slides and choreograph a seamless cinematic flow from one point to the next.

- **Accessing the Animation Pane**

The hub for controlling animations and transitions in Keynote is the handy Animation pane, which can be displayed by selecting **View > Animation** in the menu bar. This pane provides quick access to all the motion effects you can apply to objects and slides.

You can also find animation controls by right-clicking any object and choosing **"Animate"** from the contextual menu. This method automatically binds the effects you choose to that specific element.

- **Intro Animation Effects**

One of the most common uses for animations is dictating how objects appear on each slide during your presentation. You can apply simple entrance effects like fades, dissolves or wipes to have elements gently materialize on the screen.

However, Keynote also offers more dynamic "build" animations that introduce objects individually with moves, rotations, and other eye-catching styles. It is perfect for unveiling bullet points or sequentially highlighting different components of a diagram in visual story form.

- **Emphasis and Motion Path Effects**

In addition to intros, you can animate objects to add emphasis and focused attention at crucial moments. Some simple emphasis effects include gently pulsing, spinning, bouncing or even handwriting animations to mimic drawing out an illustration live.

Explore Keynote's motion path animations for more advanced visuals, which allow you to choreograph custom movement patterns for objects across the slide canvas. You could create visual flows between connected elements or have an object icon follow the path of an example you're describing.

- **Slide Transition Styles**

Of course, no discussion of motion effects would be complete without exploring Keynote's extensive library of slide transition styles. These dictate the animated treatment during presentation mode as you advance from one slide to the next.

The transitions range from simple fade polygons and wipe effects to more dynamic 3D cube spin animations that can create a layered blockbuster movie vibe. Each transition style includes controls to

macOS Sonoma User's Guide

adjust the duration and direction for a fully customized experience.

- **Magic Move Transitions**

For those who want to take their transition game to the next level, explore Keynote's Magic Move feature. It allows you to link objects across consecutive slides so that animations flow seamlessly from one to the next.

For example, you could have an introductory title image on slide one grow and transform it into an exploded diagram visual on slide two. Or you might choreograph a presenter move across separate slide canvases to maintain continuous motion while the background scene changes.

- **Adjustment and Preview Controls**

No matter which types of animations you opt to use, Keynote provides plenty of tools to fine-tune the effect timing and playback. The built-in preview mode allows you to scrub through animations across all slides to check your choreography.

You can also apply adjustment controls like start and end triggers, repeating the behavior, and delays to ensure objects and transitions play precisely how you want them to. These refinements help sell the production value of your presentation delivery.

Present Your Slideshow on a Screen or Share it Online

You've crafted a visually stunning, motion-rich presentation using all the powerful tools in Keynote on your Mac. But your work isn't over until you've delivered that slideshow to its intended audience. Thankfully, Keynote provides several flexible options for presenting live or sharing online, ensuring your story always shines through.

- **Presenting on an External Display**

You'll likely want to connect your Mac to a larger screen or projector for maximum impact for in-person presentations. Keynote's presenter display mode makes this a seamless experience. Connect your secondary display, then click the Play button in the toolbar (or use the Play Slideshow keyboard shortcut).

Your Mac's built-in display will show the presenter view with upcoming slide previews, notes, and navigation controls. At the same time, your presentation plays full-screen on the external monitor. You can customize the displays to show or hide elements like the timer, current slide number, and mirroring options.

- **Recording Your Voice**

You'll want to use Keynote's built-in voice recording feature for virtual presentations or pre-recorded videos. It lets you capture a seamless voiceover narration timed precisely to your slideshow animations and builds.

To access recording controls, go to the Play menu and select **"Record Slideshow."** You can choose whether to record the entire presentation or rehearse sections, and the app will guide you through the process using your Mac's microphone. Recorded audio files are embedded into your Keynote document for easy playback or export.

- **Sharing Online**

You may need to share your presentations across remote locations without the burden of additional file transfers. Keynote simplifies this process with its "Share" menu that allows you to transmit your slideshows directly through popular online channels.

For example, you can quickly generate a public iCloud link to grant anyone with the URL temporary access to view or download your presentation. Keynote also integrates with cloud services like Box and Dropbox for sharing through those platforms.

If you have an Apple TV nearby, you can even use AirPlay to beam your live Keynote presentation wirelessly to a TV display. Enter AirPlay server mode, and your Mac will automatically detect compatible Apple TV receivers on the local network.

- **Exploring Different Export Options**

Sometimes, you'll need to package your keynote presentation in a specific file format to share with those who may not have the app installed. Thankfully, Keynote supports a wide variety of export formats from its File > Export menu:

PDF: For printable slide handouts or static document viewing

PowerPoint: Compatible with Microsoft's ubiquitous presentation software

HTML: Publish entire web-based slideshows that can be viewed in any browser

Images: Export individual slides or the whole deck as image files

QuickTime/MP4: Create video renderings of your animated presentations

There are plenty of customization settings to adjust visual quality, including speaker notes, show skipped slides, and more when generating exports.

- **Remote Presentation on Displays and TVs**

A new feature in macOS Sonoma is presenting your Keynote slideshows remotely on other displays and smart TVs using your iPhone or iPad. After installing the latest software update, select the **"Present Remotely"** option from Keynote's Play menu.

Your Mac will automatically scan for nearby AirPlay or cloud-linked displays and let you beam your presentation with just a few taps. You can customize the appearance with professional remote pointer tools from your iOS device.

CHAPTER FOURTEEN

Apple Music

The first step to Apple Music is to set it up on your Mac. With macOS Sonoma, the process is streamlined and intuitive. Launch the Music app (you can find it in the Applications folder or use Spotlight search), and you'll be greeted with the option to sign in with your Apple ID. If you don't have an Apple ID yet, no worries. You can easily create one during the setup process.

Once signed in, Apple Music will prompt you to subscribe to the service. Choose the plan that suits your needs, and you'll gain immediate access to the vast Apple Music library, personalized playlists, and exclusive content.

Navigating the Apple Music Interface

The Apple Music interface on macOS Sonoma is both visually appealing and user-friendly. The sidebar on the left provides quick access to various sections, including Library, Playlists, Radio, and more. The main window displays featured content, albums, playlists, and personalized recommendations based on your listening history and preferences.

To find your favorite artists or albums, use the top search bar. You can also browse through curated playlists based on genres, moods, or activities. Apple Music's intelligent algorithms continuously learn your tastes, ensuring your recommendations are always on point.

- **Building Your Library and Playlists**

One of the significant features of Apple Music is the ability to build your library and create personalized playlists. As you listen to songs, click the "+" button to add them to your library. You can then organize your music into playlists based on genres, moods, or any other criteria you prefer.

To create a new playlist, click the **"+" button** in the Playlists section of the sidebar, name it, and add songs. You can also share your playlists with friends and family, allowing them to enjoy your curated musical selections.

Exploring Apple Music Radio

Apple Music Radio is a fantastic way to discover new music and stay up-to-date with the latest releases. Tune in to Beats 1, Apple's global radio station, or explore a wide range of genre-specific and artist-hosted stations.

You can create your custom radio station based on a specific song, artist, or genre. Apple Music's algorithms will continuously play similar tracks, introducing you to new artists and expanding your musical horizons.

- **Accessing Apple Music Across Devices**

One of the significant advantages of Apple Music is its seamless integration across all your devices. Whether you're listening on your Mac, iPhone, iPad, or Apple TV, your library, playlists, and listening history sync automatically through iCloud; this means you can pick up where you left off, no matter your device.

With macOS Sonoma's Continuity features, you can effortlessly hand off your music playback between your Mac and your iPhone or iPad. Bring your iOS device close to your Mac, and you'll see a prompt to continue listening on your chosen device.

Apple TV+

Launch the TV app (you can find it in the Applications folder or use Spotlight search), and you'll be greeted with the option to sign in with your Apple ID. If you don't have an Apple ID yet, no worries! You can easily create one during the setup process.

Once signed in, you'll have the opportunity to subscribe to Apple TV+. Choose the plan that suits your needs, and you'll gain immediate access to a vast library of premium content, including critically acclaimed originals and curated selections from across the entertainment spectrum.

- **Navigating the Apple TV+ Interface**

The Apple TV+ interface on macOS Sonoma is sleek, intuitive, and designed to provide an immersive viewing experience. The sidebar on the left allows you to quickly access different sections, including Apple TV+, Movies, TV Shows, and more. The main window displays featured content, curated collections, and personalized recommendations based on your viewing history and preferences.

To find your favorite shows or movies, use the top search bar. You can also browse genre-specific collections, discover new releases, or explore curated lists tailored to your tastes.

- **Building Your Watchlist and Managing Subscriptions**

One of the vital features of Apple TV+ is the ability to build your watchlist and manage your subscriptions seamlessly. As you discover new shows or movies that pique your interest, click the "+" button to add them to your watchlist. It ensures your favorite content is always within reach and ready to enjoy whenever possible.

Additionally, Apple TV+ allows you to manage your subscriptions with ease. You can explore different channel subscriptions, such as premium networks or specialized streaming services, and add them to your Apple TV+ experience. This centralized platform simplifies your viewing journey, consolidating all your subscriptions in one convenient location.

macOS Sonoma User's Guide

- **Apple TV+ Originals and Exclusives**

Apple TV+ is renowned for its critically acclaimed original series and exclusive content. From gripping dramas to mind-bending sci-fi shows, there's something for every taste. Immerse yourself in the cinematic brilliance of award-winning movies, or delve into thought-provoking documentaries that shed light on fascinating topics.

With macOS Sonoma's integration, you can enjoy these premium originals and exclusives in stunning quality, with support for advanced video and audio formats, ensuring an unparalleled viewing experience.

Apple Books

Launch the Books app (you can find it in the Applications folder or use Spotlight search), and you'll be greeted with the option to sign in with your Apple ID. If you don't have an Apple ID, you can easily create one during setup.

Once signed in, you'll have access to the vast Apple Books library, where you can browse, purchase, and download a wide range of e-books, audiobooks, and more. Whether you prefer to read on your Mac's vibrant display or listen to audiobooks on the go, Apple Books has you covered.

Navigating the Apple Books Interface

The Apple Books interface on macOS Sonoma is sleek, visually appealing, and designed to enhance your reading experience. The sidebar on the left allows you to quickly access different sections, including your Library, Book Store, Audiobooks, and more. The main window displays featured content, curated collections, and personalized recommendations based on your reading history and preferences.

To find your favorite books or authors, use the top search bar. You can also browse genre-specific collections, discover new releases, or explore curated lists tailored to your tastes.

macOS Sonoma User's Guide

- **Building Your Digital Library**

With Apple Books, you can build and manage your digital library seamlessly. As you discover new books pique your interest, click the "Buy" or "Get" button to add them to your library. Apple Books supports many e-book formats, ensuring you can easily access your favorite titles.

Additionally, you can organize your library into collections based on genres, authors, or any other criteria you prefer. This customizable organization system keeps your digital library neat and easily accessible.

- **Immersive Reading Experience**

Apple Books on macOS Sonoma offers an immersive reading experience that caters to your preferences. With the built-in reader, you can adjust the font size, brightness, and background color to create the perfect reading environment. You can also take advantage of features like night mode, which reduces eye strain during late-night reading sessions.

If you love audiobooks, Apple Books provides a seamless listening experience. You can adjust the playback speed, set a sleep timer, and even create bookmarks to pick up where you left off effortlessly.

Podcasts

The Apple Podcasts app is a beautiful way to discover, subscribe to, and listen to your favorite podcasts on your Mac. With macOS Sonoma, Apple has redesigned the podcast experience to be more immersive and intuitive.

- **Accessing Apple Podcasts**

You can easily access the Podcasts app on your Mac by searching for it in the Spotlight menu or the Applications folder. For quick access, I recommend pinning it to your Dock by right-clicking on the app icon and selecting **"Keep in Dock."**

macOS Sonoma User's Guide

- **Browsing and Subscribing**

Upon opening Podcasts, you're greeted by a clean, magazine-style layout that immediately immerses you in new and popular podcasts to explore. As you scroll through carousels of featured shows, gorgeous artwork and enticing episode descriptions draw you in. When an exciting podcast catches your eye, click the **"Subscribe"** button to follow it.

- **Your Library and Stations**

All of your subscribed podcasts are neatly organized in your Library. Here, you can quickly browse new episodes as they're released and download the ones you want to save for offline listening. For a steady stream of episodes tailored to your tastes, check out the **"Stations"** feature, which curates a continuous playlist based on your subscriptions and listening habits.

- **Playback and Controls**

Double-clicking an episode launches the sleek player interface. Keyboard controls allow you to play/pause, skip, adjust volume, and more without leaving your keyboard. You can even ask Siri to play specific podcasts. As you listen, live transcripts sync with the audio, allowing you to reference crucial moments quickly.

For example, skim the transcripts to find it instantly instead of manually scrubbing through the audio if you're following a true crime podcast and want to jump back to catch a crucial quote.

- **Cross-Device Syncing**

One of the best perks of Podcasts on macOS is seamless multi-device syncing through iCloud. Start an episode on your Mac, and you can pick up where you left off on your iPhone, iPad or Apple TV. Your playback position, subscriptions, and downloaded episodes roam with you across all your Apple devices.

macOS Sonoma User's Guide

One unique new Sonoma feature is the ability to create **RSS feeds** from your subscriptions. It allows you to share custom podcast stations or playlists with friends or keep an updated feed of all your latest episodes synced to your devices outside the Podcasts app.

Apple Arcade

The Apple Arcade app brings an entire world of amazing games to your Mac. With macOS Sonoma, Apple has leveled up the Arcade experience with exciting new features that will delight casual players and hardcore gamers alike.

- **Finding Apple Arcade**

You can quickly access the Apple Arcade app from the Applications folder, Launchpad, or by spotlighting it with a quick Cmd+Space search. I recommend pinning it to your Dock by right-clicking the icon and selecting Options > Keep in Dock for easy access.

- **Browsing and Downloading Games**

When you first open Arcade, you're greeted by a sleek, full-screen interface optimized for gaming. Browse gorgeous tiled previews of every game in the catalog across categories like Awards, Indie Hits, Action, Platformers, and more. With rich metadata and video trailers just a click away, it's easy to get excited about your next gaming adventure. Downloading a game is as simple as clicking the iridescent sidebar button.

- **Your Game Library**

All your downloaded Arcade games are automatically organized into a clean Library view. You can jump back into recently played titles or start fresh adventures with a click. Arcade keeps your game progress and achievements and saves synchronized across all your devices through iCloud.

For example, if you start a game at home on your iMac and need to take a break, you can instantly

macOS Sonoma User's Guide

pick up from the same spot later on your iPad or iPhone.

- **Controller Support and Settings**

While many Arcade games are perfectly playable with a keyboard/mouse or trackpad, the app also provides full native support for various controllers and arcade sticks. Connect your preferred gamepad, and Arcade will automatically map the buttons. You can even customize your control layout on a per-game basis through the app's settings menu.

- **Game Center Integration**

Apple Arcade integrates directly with Game Center on Sonoma if you love friendly competition. You can track achievements, view leaderboards, and even challenge friends to beat your high scores right from within the app. Smack-talking is optional but highly encouraged.

One unique new feature in macOS Sonoma is creating sharable game libraries from your downloaded Arcade collection. It allows you to easily share your favorite game lineup with family members or friends to try out. It's a great way to socialize your gaming habits or discover new titles through people you trust.

iCloud+

Apple's iCloud service has always been an excellent way to synchronise your documents, photos, and other data across all your devices. With iCloud+ on macOS Sonoma, this cloud storage solution is leveling up with robust new privacy and collaboration features that will change how you think about cloud computing.

- **Enabling iCloud+**

Getting started with iCloud+ is very straightforward. Open the System Settings app, click on your Apple ID at the top, and select "iCloud" from the sidebar. If you're not already subscribed, you can sign up for any paid iCloud storage plans here. Once subscribed, check the "iCloud+" box to unlock the suite of new data privacy services.

- **Private Relay**

One of the marquee features of iCloud+ is Private Relay, which encrypts all your Safari browsing data and routes it through two separate internet relays to obscure your traffic from networks and websites. It ensures your online activities remain private and anonymous without sacrificing performance. You can enable Private Relay from the iCloud menu and even choose an IP address location.

- **Hide My Email**

Another great iCloud+ tool is the ability to generate unlimited randomized email addresses to use with online accounts, newsletters, and more. The **"Hide My Email"** feature lets you hand out pseudo-anonymous addresses that forward to your private inbox, shielding your actual email from potential spam and tracking. Creating aliases is easy - click the "Hide My Email" button whenever you need to share an email address online.

- **ICloud Private Clipboard**

Have you ever copied sensitive text or login credentials on one device, only to try pasting it hours later, and wondered why it didn't sync to the clipboard on your other devices? iCloud Private Clipboard solves this by allowing you to copy once and paste across all synced devices, using end-to-end encryption to protect your copied data until you need it again.

- **ICloud Shared Photo Library**

In addition to privacy features, iCloud+ also delivers new ways to collaborate through the cloud. The Shared Photo Library lets you create an entirely separate iCloud photo stream to share with up to 5 others. Everyone can add their photos, videos and comments in one unified library that intelligently syncs across everyone's devices.

macOS Sonoma User's Guide

For example, if you created a Shared Photo Library for an upcoming family reunion, you could all upload your photos and videos from the event into one centralized place to view and relive those memories together.

One unique new component of iCloud+ on Sonoma is automatically uploading photos or documents stored in your iCloud Drive to a private, encrypted CloudSafe vault. This vault uses advanced cryptography to protect your most sensitive data with an extra layer of security that even Apple cannot access. It's the perfect place to store essential records, financial documents, or anything else you want to be kept ultra-private.

CHAPTER FIFTEEN

Keep macOS Sonoma Secure

Keeping your Mac safe from cyber threats is crucial in today's digital world. With macOS Sonoma, Apple has introduced robust security features to protect your data and privacy.

- **Enable System Integrity Protection**

System Integrity Protection (SIP) is a robust security measure that prevents unauthorized modifications

macOS Sonoma User's Guide

to critical system files and processes. To activate SIP, follow these steps:

Restart your Mac and immediately press and hold the Command + R keys to enter Recovery Mode.

Once in Recovery Mode, select "Utilities" from the menu bar and choose "Terminal."

In the Terminal window, type csrutil status to check SIP's current status.

If SIP is disabled, enter csrutil enable and press Return. Your Mac will restart with SIP enabled.

SIP acts as a gatekeeper, preventing even root-level processes from altering protected system files and directories. This defense mechanism thwarts potential malware attacks and ensures the integrity of your macOS installation.

- **Keep Your Software Up-to-Date**

Regularly updating your Mac's software is a simple yet effective way to maintain a secure system. Apple promptly releases security patches and updates to address vulnerabilities and emerging threats. Here's how to ensure your Mac stays up-to-date:

Click on the Apple menu and select "System Settings."

Choose "Software Update" and click "Update Now" to install any available updates.

Enable automatic updates by checking the "Automatically keep my Mac up to date" option.

For instance, a recent security update addressed a critical vulnerability in the Safari web browser that could allow remote code execution. Keeping your software up-to-date ensures that such vulnerabilities are promptly patched, minimizing the risk of exploitation.

- **Use Strong and Unique Passwords**

Weak or reused passwords are a common entry point for cybercriminals. macOS Sonoma includes advanced password management tools to help you create and store strong, unique passwords for each account and service you use.

Open the Safari browser and navigate to a website or app that requires a password.

When prompted to enter a password, click the "Suggest New Password" option.

Safari will generate a strong, random password that you can use for that account.

Choose "Save Password" to store the password securely in your iCloud Keychain.

Using unique, complex passwords for each account significantly reduces the risk of unauthorized access, even if one of your passwords is compromised. iCloud Keychain syncs your passwords across all your Apple devices, ensuring secure access to your accounts from anywhere.

- **Enable Firewall Protection**

macOS Sonoma's built-in firewall monitors incoming and outgoing network connections, blocking unauthorized access attempts. To activate the firewall:

Open System Settings and navigate to "Network."

Click on "Firewall" and toggle the switch to turn it on.

Choose "Firewall Options" to customize settings, such as allowing specific apps to receive incoming connections.

With the firewall enabled, you can rest assured that your Mac is protected from network-based threats, such as unauthorized remote access attempts or malicious traffic. This added layer of security ensures that only trusted applications and services can communicate over your network.

- **Use FileVault to Encrypt Your Data**

FileVault is a powerful encryption tool that protects your data from unauthorized access, even if your Mac is lost or stolen. Here's how to enable FileVault:

Open System Settings and go to "Privacy & Security."

Select "FileVault" and click "Turn On FileVault."

Follow the prompts to create a recovery key and enable disk encryption.

With FileVault enabled, your Mac's entire disk is encrypted, safeguarding your files, documents, and personal information from prying eyes. Even if someone gains physical access to your Mac, they won't be able to access your data without the correct encryption key.

- **Stay Vigilant Against Phishing Attempts**

Phishing attacks are a common tactic cybercriminals use to steal sensitive information or gain unauthorized access to your accounts. macOS Sonoma includes built-in protection against phishing attempts, but it's essential to remain vigilant.

Be cautious of unsolicited emails or messages, especially those containing links or attachments.

Hover over links to verify the destination URL before clicking.

If an email or message seems suspicious, don't engage – delete or report it immediately.

For instance, a phishing email might claim to be from your bank and ask you to update your account information by clicking a malicious link. By staying vigilant and verifying the legitimacy of such requests, you can avoid falling victim to these deceptive tactics.

Utilizing the Accessibility Features

Apple has made great strides in making its operating systems more accessible for users with disabilities or impairments. macOS Sonoma builds on this with new and enhanced accessibility features to empower all users.

- **Getting Started**

Before we explore the accessibility features, you'll need to open the Accessibility preferences pane. You can find this by going to the **Apple menu >**

System Preferences > Accessibility or using the keyboard shortcut Control + Option + F. The Accessibility pane lets you turn features on or off and customize their settings.

- **Vision Accessibility**

Sonoma has powerful tools for users with low or impaired vision to increase visibility and clarity. VoiceOver is a built-in screen reader that can describe your screen's content aloud. You can customize its voice, verbosity levels, and navigation controls.

Zoom allows you to enlarge portions of the screen up to 20 times their average size using keyboard shortcuts or gesture controls. The new Picture Cursor makes it easier to track the pointer with a high-contrast outline.

- **Hearing and Audio Assistance**

The new Live Listen feature helps users with hearing impairments by using the iPhone or iPad microphone as a remote mic that funnels sound directly to your Mac. You can focus on voices in front of you while minimizing background noise.

Sonic HDMI enhances audio clarity on Macs with compatible HDMI video cards. It can isolate voice frequencies to make dialogue crisper and easier to understand when watching videos.

- **Motor Skills Assistance**

For those with physical motor disabilities, Sonoma introduces the Address Keys feature. It converts uppercase letter combinations like CMD+N into more straightforward one-handed key sequences. You can also enable Sticky Keys to combine key presses instead of chording them.

The updated Dictation tool uses advanced speech recognition to let you edit text and interact with your Mac using just your voice. It incorporates new voice control capabilities for commands like switching between apps and tabs.

- **Cognitive Assistance**

Sonoma includes assistive tools for users with cognitive disabilities or neurodivergence, like ADHD and autism. Focus Filters adjust lighting and color values to increase clarity and minimize visual distraction. You can customize filters for specific apps or tasks.

The innovative Guided Tour feature walks you through apps and processes using descriptive prompts and highlighting relevant buttons. It creates an immersive tutorial experience catered to your pace and learning needs.

CHAPTER SIXTEEN

Use a Printer on Your macOS Sonoma

The first step to printing is connecting your printer to your Mac. With macOS Sonoma, this process is delightfully simple. Plug in your printer using the appropriate cable (USB, Ethernet, or wireless connection), and your Mac should automatically

macOS Sonoma User's Guide

detect and configure it. If not, open the System Settings app, navigate to "Printers & Scanners," and follow the prompts to add your printer manually.

- **Install Printer Software (If needed)**

Some printers require additional software or drivers to be installed. Check your printer's documentation or the manufacturer's website for instructions. macOS Sonoma often includes pre-installed drivers for popular printer models. However, having the latest software ensures optimal performance and access to advanced features.

- **The Print Dialog**

Once your printer is set up, printing is a breeze. Open the document, image, or file you want to print, and use the "File" menu or the Command+P keyboard shortcut to access the Print dialog. Here, you can select your printer, choose the number of copies, adjust the page range, and tinker with various printing options.

- **Customizing Your Print Job**

The Print dialog offers a wealth of customization options. Depending on your printer's capabilities, you can adjust paper size, orientation, scaling, and quality settings. Want to print multiple pages on a single sheet? No problem! Need to save ink? Select the "Grayscale" or "Black & White" option. These settings ensure your printouts look precisely the way you want them.

- **Previewing and Printing**

Before committing your document to paper, use the handy Preview feature. It shows precisely how your printout will look, allowing you to catch any formatting issues or make last-minute adjustments. Once satisfied, click the "Print" button, and your Mac will send the job to your printer, bringing your digital content to life on paper.

While macOS Sonoma offers a fantastic printing experience out of the box, Apple continuously innovates to enhance this essential feature. Stay

macOS Sonoma User's Guide

tuned for updates that may introduce new printing technologies, improved efficiency, or tighter integration with your favorite apps and cloud services.

Connect to Wi-Fi

One of the most convenient features of macOS Sonoma is its ability to connect to known Wi-Fi networks automatically. Once you've connected to a network, your Mac remembers its credentials and reconnects (automatically) whenever you're in range. You can move between your home, office, and favorite coffee shops without missing a beat.

- **Joining New Networks**

To connect to a new Wi-Fi network, click the Wi-Fi icon in the menu bar and select the desired network from the list. If the network is password-protected, macOS Sonoma will prompt you to enter the password. Fear not if you're unsure of the password – many routers now feature a handy QR code that your Mac can scan for instant connectivity.

- **Wi-Fi Preferences**

For more advanced options, open the System Settings app and navigate to the "Wi-Fi" section. Here, you can view a list of available networks, their signal strengths, and security settings. You can also join hidden networks, prioritize preferred networks, and configure advanced settings like proxies or VLAN tags.

- **Wi-Fi Diagnostics**

If you're experiencing connectivity issues, macOS Sonoma's Wi-Fi Diagnostics tool can be a lifesaver. This utility scans for potential problems, analyzes your network environment, and provides detailed information to help you troubleshoot and resolve any issues. It's like having a personal Wi-Fi expert at your fingertips.

macOS Sonoma User's Guide

- **Wi-Fi Sharing and Hotspot**

In addition to connecting to existing networks, macOS Sonoma allows you to share your Mac's internet connection with other devices. Enable "Internet Sharing" in System Settings, and your Mac will create a personal Wi-Fi hotspot to which other devices can connect. This feature is perfect for when you need to stay productive on the go or share your internet connection with friends or colleagues.

Use an External Display

The first step towards embracing a multi-display setup is connecting your external display to your Mac. Depending on your display and Mac model, you can use various connections such as HDMI, DisplayPort, Thunderbolt, or USB-C. Plug in the appropriate cable, and your Mac should automatically detect the external display.

- **Configuring Display Settings**

Once your external display is connected, navigate to System Settings's "Displays" section to fine-tune your setup. Here, you can arrange your displays, adjust resolution, and even enable features like display mirroring or display extension, which allows you to treat your external display as an independent workspace.

- **Desktop Expansion**

With display extension enabled, your desktop seamlessly extends across multiple displays, providing a vast digital canvas. Imagine having your email client, web browser, and productivity apps open simultaneously, each occupying its own dedicated space – no more constant window juggling or minimizing.

- **Window Management**

macOS Sonoma's window management features work hand-in-hand with external displays, allowing you to move windows between screens with a simple drag-and-drop or keyboard shortcut. You can even create custom window layouts tailored to your workflow, ensuring your applications are always positioned precisely where you need them.

- **Optimized for Creativity**

For creative professionals, external displays can be a true game-changer. Designers, photographers, and videographers can take advantage of the added screen real estate to view their projects in full detail while keeping tools and palettes organized on a separate display. This setup eliminates the need for constant window switching, allowing for a more immersive and efficient creative process.

Get help with your Mac

- **The Help Menu**

The Help menu is located in the menu bar at the top of your screen, providing quick access to a comprehensive library of articles, tutorials, and troubleshooting guides explicitly tailored to your app.

- **Siri for Mac**

Siri, Apple's intelligent virtual assistant, is now more powerful than ever on macOS Sonoma. With a simple voice command or keyboard shortcut, you can summon Siri and ask for help with various tasks, from finding specific system settings to troubleshooting common issues. Siri's natural language processing ensures your queries are understood and answered accurately.

- **Apple Support Website**

Apple's online Support website is a treasure trove of information for Mac users. You'll find extensive knowledge bases, user guides, and step-by-step tutorials covering numerous topics, from basic setup and navigation to advanced tips and tricks. The site also features a vibrant community forum where you can ask questions, share experiences, and learn from fellow Mac enthusiasts.

macOS Sonoma User's Guide

- **Apple Support App**

For a more personalized experience, consider downloading the Apple Support app from the App Store. This powerful tool allows you to search for solutions, schedule repair appointments, and even initiate remote support sessions with Apple's certified technicians. The app also provides proactive notifications and updates, ensuring you're always up-to-date on the latest software releases and security patches.

- **Apple Authorized Service Providers**

In cases where you require hands-on assistance, macOS Sonoma makes it easy to locate nearby Apple Authorized Service Providers. These certified professionals are trained to handle diverse Mac-related issues, from hardware repairs to data recovery. With Apple's robust network of service providers, you can rest assured that expert help is never far away.

Identifying and Resolving Common Issues on Your macOS

No matter how reliable your Mac is, you're bound to run into issues with macOS Sonoma occasionally. But don't worry - most common problems have straightforward solutions if you know where to look. This guide will empower you to diagnose and resolve many typical macOS Sonoma issues confidently.

- **Identifying the Problem**

The first step is to pinpoint what's going wrong. Is an app crashing? Is your Mac running slowly? Are you unable to connect to a network? Carefully observe any error messages, sluggish behavior, or other symptoms. It will help narrow down the potential causes.

- **Restarting to Refresh**

Sometimes, the simplest solution is the most effective. Restart your Mac to clear any temporary glitches or frozen states causing issues. Think of it like rebooting your brain after a mental logjam.

To restart, click the **Apple icon > Restart**. Or use the keyboard shortcut Control+Command+Power button.

- **App-Specific Troubleshooting**

If a particular app seems to be the culprit, start there. Many apps have built-in utilities to clear caches, reset preferences, or repair permissions.

For example, if Safari is acting up:

Quit Safari (Command+Q)

Go to Safari > Clear History and Website Data

Restart Safari

It clears any corrupt caches or data that could gum up the works.

- **Software Updates**

Ensuring your apps and operating system are up-to-date is crucial. Apple regularly releases patches and updates to fix known bugs and security vulnerabilities.

To check for updates:

Go to System Preferences > Software Update

Click "Update Now" if any critical updates are available

You can also set your Mac to install updates automatically for seamless maintenance.

- **Kernel Panics and Crashes**

A kernel panic is an operating system crisis - your Mac's Version of throwing its hands up in exasperation. The culprit is often a software conflict, corrupt file, or hardware issue.

First, restart in Safe Mode to isolate the problem:

Restart your Mac and immediately hold Shift

Release Shift when the Apple logo appears

Your Mac will run a directory check and load only the required kernels

If all seems well in Safe Mode, restart normally and troubleshoot software conflicts. But if problems persist, you may have a hardware issue that requires professional service.

- **Managing Storage**

Is your startup disk almost filled? Performance will suffer as open space dwindles. Use the Storage Management tool to optimize usage:

Go to About This Mac > Storage

The tool analyzes and recommends ways to save space

Options may include storing files in iCloud, removing old backups and caches, etc.

Give your Mac some breathing room to function better.

- **When All Else Fails - Reset**

Suppose you've exhausted all other options, and your Mac remains unstable or wonky. In that case, you may need to reset or reinstall macOS as a final measure.

Back up any critical data first using Time Machine or iCloud. Then:

Restart in Recovery Mode (hold Command+R at startup)

In the Utilities window, select "Reinstall macOS."

Follow the onscreen instructions to reinstall a fresh copy

This nuclear option nukes any software conflicts or corruption causing problems but maintains your data.

Using the Built-In Troubleshooting Tools

When your Mac starts acting up, don't panic - Apple has equipped macOS Sonoma with a robust set of built-in troubleshooting utilities. These handy tools can diagnose and resolve many common

macOS Sonoma User's Guide

issues, getting your system back on track with minimal hassle.

- **Accessing the Utilities**

Depending on your needs, there are a few different ways to access the troubleshooting tools. Go to System Preferences > View > Troubleshooting for general maintenance and basic fixes. It opens the centralized Troubleshooting dashboard.

If you need to boot into a specialized recovery environment to tackle more severe software issues, restart while holding Command+R. It loads the Recovery Mode utilities.

You must enter Apple Diagnostics by restarting and holding D while your Mac reboots for deep hardware diagnostics and repairs.

- **General Troubleshooting**

You'll find a suite of tools for analyzing and resolving common software problems in the Troubleshooting preference pane. Here are a few key ones to try:

Restart in Safe Mode - This boots your Mac with only essential kernel extensions and fonts loaded, isolating potential software conflicts.

Reset NVRAM/PRAM - Resets specific system settings like screen resolution, disk settings, and speaker volume that may have become corrupted.

Repair Disk Permissions - Verifies and repairs disk permissions on your startup volume to fix file access issues.

The pane provides quick access to apps like Console for viewing system logs, Activity Monitor for managing processes, and Disk Utility for disk repairs and maintenance.

- **Recovery Mode Toolkit**

When booted into Recovery Mode, you have access to a prevailing set of tools for dealing with deeper software issues:

macOS Sonoma User's Guide

Reinstall macOS - Performs a fresh, clean installation of the latest version without affecting your data;

Safari - A primary web browser for looking up support info and downloading other tools if needed;

Disk Utility - For verifying, repairing, erasing, and managing disks and disk images;

Terminal - Provides command-line access to run advanced Unix tools and scripts.

- **Hardware Diagnostics and Repair**

If you suspect a hardware problem, boot into Apple Diagnostics mode to run a full suite of tests on your Mac's components like the logic board, memory, wireless modules, and more.

The tools will isolate any issues and guide necessary repairs. Apple-certified technicians can then complete those repairs or replacements using this diagnostic info.

- **Built for Troubleshooting Success**

Apple recognizes that even the most reliable systems can occasionally run into snags. That's why they've baked such a predominant set of troubleshooting tools into macOS Sonoma.

Tips and Tricks on macOS Sonoma

Apple's latest desktop operating system, macOS Sonoma, has new features and enhancements that can streamline your workflow and boost productivity.

- **Introducing Focus Filters**

One of Sonoma's standout features is Focus Filters, which allows you to create custom filters for apps and websites based on your current activity. To access Focus Filters, click the Control Center icon in the menu bar, select "Focus," and create a new Focus. For instance, you can set up a "Work" Focus

macOS Sonoma User's Guide

that blocks distracting websites and only shows work-related apps.

- **Desktop Level**

Have you ever wished you could group related windows on your desktop? With Desktop Level, you can do just that. To use this feature, hover your cursor over the green "full screen" button in any window, then select "Desktop Level" from the menu. It creates a dedicated desktop space for that app's windows, keeping your workspace tidy.

- **Live Captions**

Whether watching a video or participating in a video call, Live Captions can be a game-changer. Enable Live Captions from the Control Center, and macOS will automatically generate captions for audio playing on your Mac. This feature is convenient for those with hearing impairments or for situations where you need to keep the volume down.

- ## Quick Notes

Have you ever had a brilliant idea or an imperative thought while working but struggled to find a place to jot it down? Quick Notes solves this problem. Summon Quick Notes by pressing the Globe key + Q or setting up a hot corner in System Settings. You can then create a note that stays visible on your current window, ensuring your ideas are captured without disrupting your workflow.

- ## Customizing Spotlight

Spotlight, macOS's built-in search tool, has always been a powerful asset, but Sonoma takes it to new heights. You can now customize Spotlight to prioritize specific types of results, such as documents, web searches, or app suggestions, based on your preferences. This personalized approach ensures that Spotlight delivers the most relevant information for your needs.

macOS Sonoma User's Guide

- **Continuity Tethering**

With Continuity Tethering, you can seamlessly share your Mac's internet connection with other Apple devices, even when you're on the go. Enable this feature in System Settings > General > AirDrop & Tethering. It's a lifesaver when you need internet access but don't have a reliable Wi-Fi connection.

- **Mastering Dictation**

Typing can be time-consuming, especially when working on a lengthy document or email. Sonoma's Dictation feature has improved accuracy and support for more languages. To start dictating, press the Function (fn) key twice or enable the Dictation option in System Settings > Keyboard. Say goodbye to typing fatigue and embrace the power of voice input.

- **Customizing Control Center**

The Control Center in Sonoma is highly customizable, allowing you to add or remove various controls and toggles based on your preferences. To customize the Control Center, click the Control Center icon in the menu bar, then select "Customize Controls." This way, you can ensure that your most frequently used controls are just a click away.

- **Utilizing Hot Corners**

Hot Corners are a nifty feature that lets you trigger specific actions by moving your cursor to a designated corner of the screen. Set up Hot Corners in System Settings > Desktop & Dock > Hot Corners. For example, you can configure a Hot Corner to show the Desktop, open the Notification Center, or initiate a screensaver.

- **Stage Manager**

Stage Manager is a powerful window management tool that helps you stay focused by automatically organizing your open windows and apps. Enable Stage Manager from the Control Center by pressing the Control + Command + M keyboard shortcut. With a single click, you can

macOS Sonoma User's Guide

switch between different workspaces, ensuring that your desktop remains clutter-free and your attention stays on the task.

- **Live Text**

Live Text is a game-changing feature that allows you to interact with text in images or videos as if it were selectable and editable text. In Sonoma, Live Text has improved accuracy and support for more languages, making it even more useful for tasks like copying text from images or translating foreign text.

CONCLUSION

You've now reached the end of this comprehensive guide to mastering macOS Sonoma. Throughout the preceding chapters, you've learned how to get up and running with Apple's latest operating system, customize your desktop and system preferences to your liking, and take full advantage of powerful apps like Finder, Mail, Safari, Photos, and more.

However, this book has merely scratched the surface of what macOS Sonoma offers. With each new release, Apple continues to expand and refine its desktop operating system, adding innovative features while improving speed and efficiency. As you spend more time with Sonoma, you'll likely discover your favorite apps, shortcuts, and workflows.

You need not be intimidated and continue exploring. macOS rewards the curious with hidden

macOS Sonoma User's Guide

gems and productivity-enhancing capabilities around every corner. Refer to this guide whenever you need a refresher and feel empowered to go off the beaten path. After all, the best way to master any operating system is to roll up your sleeves and immerse yourself in it.

With Sonoma's intuitive design and robust underpinnings, you have a competent machine at your fingertips. Where you choose to take it from here is up to you.

ABOUT THE AUTHOR

Perry Hoover is a researcher, tech Entrepreneur, blogger and a technology writer, who is fond of blogging, technology research and writing. His areas of interest include Web application penetration testing, web security/architecture, cryptography, programming languages and database security. He is well versed with the latest technology, programming languages, computer hardware/software, and programming tools. He is also an expert in database security and application security architecture and penetration testing. He loves to share information about new technology and has published dozens of articles on it.

He has written articles on different aspects of IT Technologies including IT security, data storage and application development for magazines and has also published and co-published several e-books, of which the latest is on Windows 11. He has

macOS Sonoma User's Guide

also worked with different private agencies to provide solutions to IT problems.

Printed in Great Britain
by Amazon